CONTENTS

FOREWORD

I n the times in which we live, many around us are hurting. Some are distraught, and others are overwhelmed because of the enormous challenges of life. There is a need for help and hope in seasons when we are faced with mental, physical, emotion, and financial issues. It is true; we know that road we have traveled, but we do not know the one that is still ahead of us. As believers in Jesus Christ, our assurance comes from the words of Scripture. Here are just a few:

Fear not, for I am with you;
Be not dismayed, for I am your God.
I will strengthen you,
Yes, I will help you,
I will uphold you with My righteous right hand.
Isaiah 41:10

Let your conduct be without covetousness; be content with such things as you have. For He Himself has
said, "I will never leave you nor forsake you."
Hebrews 13:5

My brethren, count it all joy when you fall into various trials, ³ knowing that the testing of your faith
produces patience. ⁴ But let patience have *its* perfect
work, that you may be perfect and complete, lacking
nothing.
James 1:2-4

What an honor it is to write the forward for a book that
stretches over almost ten years in scope. Paul and Vera have
been on a journey together for the better part of 45 years.
Their love and life have been a picture of Christ and the
Church to those of us who have been onlookers. The author
and his wife have been a model couple to many who have
watched them grow together, travel the world together, and
serve in ministry together.

Our lives intersected in 1977. We became friends almost
immediately and have been intricately connected ever since.
This man and woman have opened their doors to countless
numbers of people for counseling, teaching, refreshment and
encouragement. Early on, Paul's tagline became, COUNT IT
ALL JOY. Before I knew where the verse was, and long before
I knew the context of the verse, Paul constantly said, regardless to the situation, COUNT IT ALL JOY!

I have seen this man walk through good times, and I have seen him walk through tough times. His life is a reflection of what it means to be a disciple of Jesus Christ. He accepts the teaching of Jesus in John 16:33

These things I have spoken to you, that in Me (Jesus) you may have peace. In the world you will have tribulation; but be of good cheer, I have overcome the world."

This book is a testimony of God's grace through some deep, dark seasons – the times that try men's souls. As you read his story and their story of God's grace, I know you will be encouraged, challenged and uplifted by his words, his emotions and his victories.

Paul, I want to thank you for taking the time to put your journey into words. Thank you for inviting us into your private and sometimes painful thoughts. This work has the potential to be a source of great encouragement and inspiration to many husbands, wives and children who care for loved ones as they walk through the difficulties of life. So know that your labor is not in vain in the Lord.

So for every conflict . . . We learn to COUNT IT ALL JOY.
Through every illness . . . We learn to COUNT IT ALL JOY.
Through days of darkness and nights of terror . . . We learn to COUNT IT ALL JOY.
Through broken relationships and misunderstood intentions . . . We learn to COUNT IT ALL JOY.

Through financial and physical loss . . . We learn to COUNT IT ALL JOY

And even through death . . . We learn to COUNT IT ALL JOY

Always your friend and brother,

Pastor Nate Brock

INTRODUCTION

I n years past I have always used the phrase "Count it all Joy" when I closed a letter or in saying goodbye to someone. More recently my present phrase is "Keep Pressing." Yet, as I reflected on the season God has brought to pass in the life of my family, I felt the urge to write about this journey. Truly words such as luck, chance, fortune-telling, and the like, have no place in the life of a true believer in Jesus Christ.

When things are going well and one has no problems, it is easy to have a bright outlook. However, when affliction and trouble arise, where does a person go for relief or help? Many turn to temporary remedies such as drugs, alcohol and also unwholesome relationships. Yet, I am thankful that Jesus is the center of my joy. I gave my life to Jesus Christ on Sunday afternoon, December 15, 1968. I became a new creation in Christ. I in turn shared Christ with Vera, my wife, and I am rejoicing that our names are in the Lamb's Book of Life.

When crises came into our lives we turned to our Savior. He is our refuge and strength; a very present help in trouble. God has undergirded, surrounded and kept us in the hollow of His hands. We learned over and over again that He is able to sustain us in the midst of crises. In caring for my wife I understood more and more what it entails being a servant.

It is my expectation that what you discover throughout the pages of this book will be encouraging. Nothing is wasted in God's economy. If Jesus could take five loaves of bread and two fish and feed a multitude, afterwards taking up twelve baskets of fragments, surely He can use the journey of my wife and me to give confidence and reassure someone else who is undergoing similar crises. Vera and I are still in the midst of God's plan. I pray that what we have placed in print will be to the praise of His glory and that each of you will gain strength through its contents.

There were many difficult situations my wife and I were challenged to face, but we were blessed to handle them. However, as time passed my wife began showing signs of forgetfulness. I began to pay closer attention to her responses and interactions, and as the months went by her forgetfulness became more noticeable. After several more episodes, she conceded to see a doctor. We were escorted to an exam room where we were approached by a clinician in a white jacket. As I sat and observed this clinician examine my wife, I perceived that things were about to change. Vera was diagnosed with dementia. Upon hearing the news I prayed, "Lord, I need your grace." A few years later I was diagnosed with a malignant salivary tumor. Yes, not only was Vera afflicted with an incurable disease, I needed medical intervention myself. As we both endure this difficult season, I am comforted to know that this did not take our great God by surprise, for it had already sifted through His tender hands. We needed only to rely as we have in the past on God and learn to experience His grace.

ACKNOWLEDGEMENT

I want to take this opportunity to express my thanks to everyone who stood and are standing in the gap for Vera and me. It is just a joy seeing the body of Christ come together to render support.

Thanks to our children: Carmela, Paul, Patrick, Renita and David have been magnanimous and considerate in caring for Vera and me. They have given of their time and resources to ensure that our needs are being met. I thank God for each of them in that they are walking in truth and allowing the Lord to use them during this season. Our youngest son, David, resides with Vera and me. He sees and experiences the everyday challenges of caregiving. I know it touches his heart very deeply, and I appreciate his being here for Vera and me. He avails himself to care for his mom, and it allows me time to do other things. Thanks David. Renita, the "general," is always on point and makes certain that all questions are answered and that we are following the regimen. She and her husband, Sam, live nearby and make sure that Vera and I do not fall "off the wagon." Patrick and Carmela come home often; Paul calls frequently to talk and check on us. I just thank God for our children who are walking in the fear of God!

Thanks to my pastor, Rev. Ossie T. Brown, Jr., and the Sanctuary church family for their countless tangible gifts, support, prayers and encouragement. Thanks to Elder Rex Snider, Lori and Dan Tennimon and the Millbrook Presbyterian Church family for their many prayers and acts of kindness. These two churches made sure we did not miss any meals.

Thanks to Sue Cobb and the Eastmont Baptist Church prayer group for scores of cards and prayers. Thanks to our friends of SPOLIWA Ministries for their benevolence, for giving words of reassurance, and praying weekly for us.

Special thanks to my mother, Ethel V. Brown, and close family members; Elaine Parks, home health nurse for taking care of Vera, me and our home; and the Wingate family for their ongoing support.

Thankfulness and gratitude is sent to those in the medical arena: primary care clinician P.A. Mumbi Gnugi; Dr. Kirk Withrow, Surgeon; Dr. Stephen L. Davidson, Hematology Oncologist and Donna Turner, OCCRNP; Dr. Michael L. Ingram, Radiation Oncologist and the radiation staff: Barbara Betts, Kendra Caudle and Chuck Lemmond; nurse Terry Blackwell who administered my chemotherapy; Julia Barlow who handled scheduling; Dr. Sara Shashy for providing neurology oversight for Vera; and the many others in the medical line of work who have played an integral part in our treatment. I appreciate their professionalism.

There were numerous individuals who contributed significantly to the care and treatment of Vera and me and for this I am ever so grateful. I praise God for putting on the hearts of so many to avail themselves to stand in the gap for us. To each of you I share this verse of Scripture: "For God is not unjust so as to forget your work and the love which would you have shown toward His name, in having ministered and in still ministering to the saints" (Hebrews 6:10, NAS).

SPECIAL ACKNOWLEDGEMENT

I pause to give special thanks and acknowledgment to my mother, Mrs. Ethel V. Brown. As I write this she just celebrated her 90th birthday. It was a real joy being with other family members and friends to rejoice and honor her. I express thanks to the Lord for giving my mother longevity of life.

My mother set the stage for me regarding being a caregiver. I observed her on numerous occasions when she cared for family members; even caring for my father before God took him home to be with Him. Mom was always the archetype of what it takes to care for others. I believe I learned a lot from her and am now employing many of those qualities I saw her model.

I observed how she earnestly, tenderly and gently attended and comforted those she cared for. I want to express appreciation for the pattern you demonstrated. You showed that when one serves from the heart it contributes significantly to the healing and restoration of the person to who care is being administered.

You, Mom, are indeed a godly and virtuous woman and I thank God for you.

Chapter 1

MY GRACE IS SUFFICIENT

"And he said unto me, My grace is sufficient for thee: for my strength is made perfect in weakness. Most gladly therefore will I rather glory in my infirmities, that the power of Christ may rest upon me." (II Corinthians 12:9)

Today, I am back at the cancer center waiting to see my hematology oncologist about my recent PET scan report. As I sit here, I reflect in the past to when this affliction occurred.

In late April of 2013, I noticed a raised area near the front of my ear along my sideburn. I was concerned so I went to a local medical facility to have it assessed. After having blood taken and the area evaluated, I was advised to go home and rest. Afterwards I contacted my primary care physician for an appointment. She sent me to have an ultrasound procedure of this raised area. The result of the ultrasound was suspicious so she ordered a CT scan. The CT scan report came back highly suspect. We discussed some possibilities as to what this raised area could be; in our discussion she shared the possibility of it being a cancerous growth. Upon hearing this news, I was very concerned. My clinician scheduled me to see an ENT physician to obtain a biopsy of the growth.

I made an appointment with ENT. My thoughts began to wander and lots of questions came to mind. The ENT physician examined me: ear, nose and throat. He placed a tube into my nose and proceeded to observe inside my nose and throat, which was a very retching experience. He proceeded to examine the raised area, took several biopsy samples, and sent it out for pathology analysis. I went home with a lot of apprehension. Vera and I left that evening for South Carolina to attend a women conference. All the time I was wondering what would be the outcome from the biopsy. The next week I returned to the ENT office for the results of the biopsy. The ENT physician came in with the report in hand and stated that the biopsy was a tumor and it is malignant for cancer. I was hoping to hear the words benign or negative. This came as a real shock to me. He stated I would need to have surgery to have the tumor removed as soon as possible. I sat back down in the chair to sort out what all I had just heard. I felt very anxious having received this news. I said to myself, "Lord, why me?" I don't smoke. I don't drink, and yet, I have a malignant tumor. The word benign was nowhere to be found.

The ENT physician recommended a surgeon at the University of Alabama in Birmingham (UAB) and made an appointment for me. I thought of Vera. Who is going to take care of her? Upon leaving the ENT office, I went to my car with a heavy heart and committed the situation to the Lord. God already knew I had a cancerous tumor, for this affliction had already sifted through His tender, loving hands. I was experiencing God's permissive will and said, "Lord, you have to take care of this because right now I do not know what to do; I look unto You." The Lord brought to my mind King Jehoshaphat. The king cried out, "If when evil come upon us and we stand before this house, and cry unto thee in our affliction, then thou wilt hear and help." When he realized that Judah was outnumbered, he turned to God, and said "..but our eyes are upon thee" (II Chronicles 20:9, 12).

I did not know what to think or expect, but I placed my situation with the God that I serve, for He has the divine ability to meet all my needs concerning this affliction. I recalled the apostle Paul prayed three times for God to remove the affliction that he was experiencing, but God's reply to him was, "My grace is sufficient for thee; for my strength is made perfect in weakness." Paul responded, "Most gladly therefore will I rather glory in my infirmities that the power of Christ may rest upon me. Therefore, I take pleasure in infirmities, in reproaches, in necessities, in persecutions, in distresses for Christ's sake; for when I am weak, then am I strong" (II Corinthians 12:9, 10). Thus, he continued proclaiming the gospel of Jesus Christ. I felt at peace knowing God has my back and His grace is sufficient. David expressed in Psalm

34:19, "Many are the afflictions of the righteous, but the Lord delivers him out of them all."

The following week my daughter, Renita, accompanied me to UAB to see Dr. Kirk Withrow. This surgeon took more biopsies to confirm the earlier report and scheduled me for surgery within two weeks. He was quite detailed and clear-cut in sharing what the team hoped to accomplish with the surgery. All of this was new to me for I had never had any type of surgery before. I kept hearing God say, "My grace is sufficient for thee."

My older daughter, Carmela, came home to stay with Vera as I prepared to return to UAB for surgery. On Wednesday morning, June 12, 2013, Renita and Sam went with me to UAB. We needed to arrive by 5 AM. I must say that it is wonderful having family support. I thank God for my children. I checked into UAB and was directed to the surgery prep area. Many thoughts were running through my mind. After getting settled into the prep area, the staff allowed Renita and Sam to visit with me until I would be taken to surgery. The nurse came over and started an IV. Renita and Sam's minister, Pastor Larry Cockrell, arrived and prayed with us. I thank God for sending him in that his prayers were a major comfort to me. Philippians 4:6-7 says, "Be careful for nothing; but in everything by prayer and supplication with thanksgiving let your requests be made known unto God. And the peace of God, which passeth all understanding, shall keep your hearts and minds through Christ Jesus." Lord, I thank you for the prayers of the body of Christ.

Soon after we prayed, the anesthesia team arrived. They answered any questions I had and then advised me that they are going to make me feel very comfortable. That was the last thing I remembered; in the next moment, I awoke in the recovery room, being told that the surgery was successful and the surgeons were pleased with the outcome. I was taken to a private room for an overnight stay. As I thought about the day's events, I recalled shaving off my beard thinking they would make an incision on the face area, but as I felt my face, to my surprise, they made the incision behind my right ear and down the neckline. I was ever so pleased. Resting and reflecting, I was making constant use of the urinal, as the IV was still running. Renita and Sam were troopers as they assisted me with lots of care. The attending surgeons came by to check on me, and said everything looked fine and that I could possibly go home in the morning. Later that night, my pastor, Rev. Ossie T. Brown, Jr., came over to find out how I was doing, and it was such a joy to see him. He was surprised to see me sitting up and talking after surgery earlier that day. I told him that God is good. He encouraged me to see that God will use this experience for His glory; that I had to experience this journey to be able to understand and minister to others who will walk this same path. He then prayed for me and the family. God started my morning with prayer and finished the day with prayer. First Thessalonians 5:17-18 says, "Pray without ceasing. In everything give thanks; for this is the will of God in Christ Jesus concerning you." I appreciated

Pastor Brown's midnight visit and praised God for the day's successful outcome.

Thursday morning after breakfast, we prepared for checkout. The staff at UAB provided me with exceptional care. I appreciated their attention and how they were concerned about my recovery. I was given meticulous instruction about the drain tubing and how to maintain it until ENT was to remove it. The attending medical assistant wheeled me towards the parking garage. Renita and Sam drove me home. Upon arriving home, Renita placed me on lockdown: in following the surgeon orders for me to rest and recover, she made it absolutely clear to me I did not do anything except rest. Now my daughter was making sure that I was obedient. I laughed as the tables were turned, and I had to listen to her. Hence, I appreciated her care and the rest of my children for them being available and contributing significantly to my recovery.

My children did not allow me to drive until a certain time that the surgeon gave clearance for me to do so. They chauffeured me if I needed to go somewhere: otherwise, I was homebound. This was a humbling experience, however I did not complain. I learned that divine intervention and human involvement went hand-in-hand. Therefore, I needed to be obedient and follow orders for my own good and well-being. My church family, Sanctuary, was also on board; for they made sure that I did not do any serving upon arrival for worship. God was looking out for me: I praised God for His goodness.

Carmela and my grandson, Lil Em, left Sunday morning for Charlotte. I truly appreciate them both being able to come home. On Monday morning the general, Renita, and Sam left to return home. I thank God they live nearby. They left me instructions not to do anything and stay inside. By Wednesday I felt like the house was closing in on me. So Vera and I stepped outside and began walking up and down the drive-way. I called Renita to advise her that her Mom and I are outside walking up and down the drive-way in case she told the neighbors to be on the lookout for the two old people next door. I thought this was funny and laughed after our conversation. The general did approve this brief time of liberty.

Vera's sister, Joy, came and stayed for a good while. She was a blessing as she assisted us during this recovery period. I just saw God's hand continually at work as he moved upon the hearts of others to serve Vera and me. She also kept the lockdown in force, following orders from Renita.

Renita accompanied me to the follow-up visit with the surgeon. She asked more questions than I did with every visit and was more inquisitive. I seemed to be taking things in stride; thank God for His peace. The post-operative visit revealed that the healing process was coming along just fine. They reassured us that they were pleased with the outcome and that I should make a full recovery. I understood more that His grace is sufficient. The surgeon gave me the green light that I could drive again and was cleared to travel. I was elated to hear this news for I desired greatly to attend the American Medical Technologist Annual Convention in Pittsburg, PA. It would be my summer to step down from serving 9 years on the board of directors.

About one month later, I returned to UAB for a follow-up appointment as I would receive consultation for radiation and possibly chemotherapy. The staff at UAB desired that I get my treatment there in Birmingham, which would be an hour away from home. My primary concern was for Vera. I thought, "Should I bring her to Birmingham? I would be getting daily treatments for radiation. How would I provide for her? It would be a new setting and nothing familiar. For a person with dementia, it is better to have a constant setting and not too many changes. At least for her it would not be in her best interest." I said, "Lord, what should I do concerning my wife? I am her caregiver? Yet I am now dealing with this medical condition that will require treatment.

However, the Lord laid it on my heart to request to be treated in Montgomery since there was a cancer center there. So they gave the approval. Again as believers, the Scriptures are our resource. It teaches us to "Ask, and it shall be given you; seek, and ye shall find; knock, and it shall be open unto you" (Matthew 7:7). So the door was opened to be treated in Montgomery. Vera could stay at home and not be subjected to travel to Birmingham. God had a purpose for allowing this infirmity. There will be others who will be used of God and integral to my recovery and Vera's care. The Lord began to move within the body of Christ to provide assistance. He did promise to supply our every need. I praise God for the system of support given by brothers and sisters in Christ. Others who were aware of our circumstances offered their support as well. Until presently, I had been using the services of a home health nurse to care for Vera on an as needed basis. However, as I would soon begin a treatment regimen, and I wondered who would I get to come and provide daily care for Vera. Elaine Parks, the home health nurse said, "Mr. Brown I will be available for as long as you need me." I praised God for her availability and again, God provided! I was prompted once more by Scripture for Peter said, "Casting all your care upon him; for He careth for you" (I Peter 5:7). Did I say God provided? Then my church family, Sanctuary, organized a meal schedule for us and provided for us so I would not be subject to do much cooking during the course of my treatment.

One day as I was leaving a printing office in Millbrook I stopped and talked with Elder Rex Snider of Millbrook Presbyterian Church. You see before now, this church has been praying for Vera due to her dementia; they were standing in the gap for us. He asked, "Brother, how are you doing?" I proceeded to share with him what had recently occurred regarding my medical condition. He asked if I would mind if he shared that with the church body. I told him that I would not mind and to please share. Later he advised me that they too would like to be of assistance to us in any way they can. So they committed to provide meals every Monday from the summer until December. God is so wonderful. I can't explain, but I can say glory hallelujah, praise His holy name! I saw the hand of God moving throughout the body of Christ.

He showed me over and over again that "My grace is sufficient for thee; for my strength is made perfect in weakness" (II Corinthians 12:9a).

The saints stood in the gap and continued in prayer for us! Provided meals for us! Called and checked on us! Gave of their substance financially to support us! Continued in prayer and gave us words of encouragement and kindness. I was scheduled for chemotherapy on Mondays. Pad Brown, the husband of my church sister Pamela, said he would be willing and available to pick me up on Mondays, stay with me during my treatment, and drive me home. This, Pad did faithfully and I appreciate his friendship and commitment. Accordingly, he availed himself and assisted me over and over again. There were others who stopped by the cancer center to encourage me while I was going through. I saw the hand of God moving on hearts and meeting our needs. His grace is sufficient.

At the Montgomery Cancer center my hematology oncologist was Dr. Stephen L. Davidson and my radiation oncologist was Dr. Michael L. Ingram. Up to this point I had only seen doctors for common colds or routine physicals, but this was all new to me. After much prayer I had to submit myself to God to use these medical professionals to meet my medical and physical needs. Dr. Davidson shared with me what he felt was the best approach to ensure that I would be treated effectively. He answered my questions regarding chemotherapy. He wanted to be certain that if any cancer cells got into circulation after surgery that they would be knocked out with the regimen of chemotherapy. He explained step by step what I could expect during the eight weeks of treatment. I was then instructed by the nursing staff about getting myself prepared, before, during and after treatments. It was very important that I eat regularly and try to maintain a high protein diet to keep my weight up. I would be reviewing all the paperwork I received that day. Preparation!

I went to see Dr. Ingram, who was very meticulous to share what his plan for radiation treatment would be for me. Again, this is all new. This would be 40 days of radiation. The chemo would last 3-4 hours; the radiation only about 10 minutes. He too instructed me to try and gain about 10 pounds because I would need it during the next 8 weeks. His nurse Barbara Betts, the radiation technicians Kendra Caudle and Church Lemmond, were all very caring and professional in their approach to treating me. They often would reassure me that things were coming along fine and to stay encouraged. When I went for radiation treatment they would have music playing; so I requested a little Motown, and they honored my request. There were days that spiritual music was also played. When I went for chemo treatment, my nurse was Terry, and she performed intravenous procedures with skilled precision. God showed He was strong on my behalf through this staff of professionals. I am thankful.

The Lord sustained me through those 8 to 9 weeks. I recalled driving up and down I-85 and would look over at the cancer center; wondering what really goes on inside this grey-looking building; now God has allowed me to see and experience what was on the inside. When receiving chemo, they would administer meds to help with nausea and I was instructed to take meds the following three days to help. Yet, there were times I experienced days of nausea. There were days I had it rather rough. While eating I felt nausea coming on and would run to the bathroom and on my knees gagging and vomiting. I would call out "My God, when is this going to be over!" Sometimes crying as I dealt with this course and still having to meet Vera's needs as her caregiver when Elaine would leave for the day.

I lost my taste for foods and began to lose weight. The staff would encourage me to try and eat a lot in order to maintain my weight. Vegetables were alright, but most meat that I ate tasted like cardboard. Joyce, Vera's other sister, advised me that I may need to process the meat in a blender so I could swallow rather than chew. I needed to keep my weight up and by-passing the meats were not helping. Subsequently, I lost between 20-25 pounds. Yet, God was most gracious, and I felt His presence each time I received treatment.

My laboratory results were dropping, and I felt myself getting weaker. However, God reminded me that His grace is sufficient for me; for my strength is made perfect in weakness." So I would pull myself up and as I always would say "Keep Pressing." I had to press my way further.

I was counting down, and. after 8-9 weeks I had my final chemo and radiation treatment. The last day finally came. I shouted, "Thank you, God!" I praise God because during this regimen I was still able to swallow and did not develop any sores within the mouth or throat that would have impeded swallowing. Even though the food began to taste horrible, I would force it down because I needed the nutrients. The milk chocolate Ensure tasted better each time.

My clothing, especially my pants, became too big due to the weight loss. I was wearing my jogging pants and washing it often; it was the only clothing that fit properly. You could pull the strings and tie it. Upon my next visit to see the surgeon at UAB, I told Renita we need to stop by the Old Navy store so I can purchase a few pants that fit.

I would see both oncologists often and they felt progress was being made. I took a PET scan and CT scan; thank God they were both negative; no cancer was seen at this time. I was scheduled for another PET scan in December; it too would come back negative. So today, February 2014, I am back for another scan report. I prayed Lord, I trust you that this too will be negative and it was. Two months ago I was a bit weak due to a decrease in my red blood cells. So I had to receive two units of blood I felt totally different afterwards; my energy level increased substantially. I praise God that the treatments were effective and presently, no sign of cancer anywhere; it is in remission. I will have to undergo future scans for a season; trusting each one to be free and negative for cancer. God is Jehovah-rappha, the Lord that healeth! I learned more and more that God's grace is sufficient. He has proven Himself over and over again to be faithful.

So today I received good news that all is well. Dr. Davidson walked into the exam room where I was writing this chapter. He said, "Why are you a healthy person among the other sick people." I rejoiced in that the good news was PET scan negative! To God be the glory. I was encouraged as I looked to my great God and Savior, thanking and praising him for all things. Thanking him for His all-sufficient grace. As I reflect on this stage of the journey, I count it all joy.

I am reminded, "For which cause we faint not; but though our outward man perish, yet the inward man is renewed day by day. For our light affliction, which is but for a moment, worketh for us a far more exceeding and eternal weight of glory" (II Corinthians 4:16-17). One gains spiritual strength and a proper perspective as a result of afflictions. Therefore, nothing is wasted in the life of a true believer. Since God knows no limit, even the affliction I experience and endure will benefit me and others.

So Lord, I thank you for your grace which is sufficient. Thank you for divine strength that I have come to realize in my human weakness; may I indeed glory in human weakness so that your power may rest upon me! Let me close this chapter with a song entitled *God's Grace* written by a dear friend and brother, Dr. Freddie C. Prince, 1989:

God's Grace

God's grace, God's grace, God's grace, for His strength is made perfect in weakness (II Corinthians 12:9).

First Stanza

Though I walk through the valley of the shadow of death;
I will fear no evil for thou art with me (Psalm 23:4).
God's grace, I said it is so sufficient.
I know what I'm talking about.
For His strength, I said is made perfect in weakness.
Shall we sin, so that grace may abound? God forbid.
I can tell you that I know His strength is made
perfect in weakness (Romans 6:1-2).

Second Stanza

Ooooo, But God is a refuge and strength.
Where we find his strength is a present help
in times of trouble (Psalm 46:1)
And know that God's grace, oooo I know that God's grace.
He is there for me and if He did it for me, He'll do it for you.
His grace is made perfect in weakness.
Seek ye first the kingdom of God and all of His righteousness,
And all these things shall be added unto you (Matthew 6:33)
I know that grace is sufficient because of what
He's done for me.
And I believe that He will do the same thing for you,
if you just trust in him.

Chapter 2

MY DIARY: DAYS IN THE LIFE OF CAREGIVING

"So teach us to number our days, that we may apply our hearts unto wisdom."(Psalm 90:12)

In this chapter I felt compelled to write about how our days have been over these past few years. I started journaling in the spring of 2011 and had no idea that God would lead me to write a book and include these diary entries as a chapter. I wanted to share with you just how the days of caregiving unfolded for me as I care for my wife, Vera, who has been diagnosed with dementia. It is a rather lengthy chapter, and I hope you can gain some insight of how I was led to handle situations with the woman I have loved for over 45 years. God is so good!

April 10, 2011

The Lord woke us up this morning; Vera had gotten up before me and was sitting on the living room sofa. I went to see if she wanted to come back to bed. The Lord gave us a good night rest. I got to bed late having worked for several hours on a sermon for Sunday morning services. Vera allowed me to help her take a shower and then I took mine. I made cereal for breakfast; she was a bit hesitant to eat, but she finally ate her breakfast. We got dressed and headed to church. We both enjoyed the Sunday school lesson and the Lord allowed me to share the morning message. Vera did well at both services. I was a bit nervous, praying she would do well. We were encouraged by our church family and returned home. I made dinner for us; David came in later. We sat on the sofa in the den, and Vera enjoyed a good time napping. We went for a 30 minute walk around 7 PM. Upon our return from walking I served her some sherbet ice cream. I hope we will have a restful night when time for bed. This is my first entry on the new laptop. I hope to keep journaling daily, as I want to reflect back on these entries in some future time. I love my wife so very much, and it pains me to see her in this way, but God knows, and I ask for wisdom daily to help her. I try to engage her in conversation often. Sometimes her reply is not on point, but I thank God for the conversation. In closing the message at church this morning I read the song "Through It All." That song sums up my feelings today. I thank God for what He is doing in our lives even during this challenging season. He is Lord of all our seasons.

April 15, 2011

The week has been quite a challenge, yet I am thankful to God for this day that He has made. Tuesday was spent preparing Vera for her colonoscopy procedure. She had to consume only clear liquids. I decided to join her in this quest. The moviprep was a real challenge because it caused her to have problems trying to get to the restroom in time. Yet, I am thankful to God as we made our way to Baptist hospital Wednesday morning. We were the first patients to arrive. They processed her in, and we waited until nursing called for her. They allowed me to accompany her to the prep room where I assisted her to get undressed and helped her put on a gown. I stayed until they took her in for her procedure. Not too long after, the clinician came out and gave me a good report that all went well. She can plan on 5-10 more years before returning again. Thank God! We returned home, and I made her some French toast with all the trimmings. She slept most of the day, resting in the den. By the evening I could not get her to sleep in the bed so she slept for a while on the sofa and spent most of the early morning doodling. Thursday was a good day. After breakfast we ran a few errands. That evening we prepared for bible study. Vera seemingly is hesitant when it comes to going to church; it takes a lot of coaching and encouraging her to remain. We returned home. She was quite tired and actually spent the whole night sleeping in the bed. I was glad. The Lord woke us up this morning. I was reading in Philippians 4 when Vera got up. I prepared breakfast for Vera and me, helped her take a shower, finished packing, and now performing a few house chores before we leave to pick up our daughter, Nita, and son-in-law, Sam, for the trip to Charleston. Pray we'll have a fruitful weekend trip and trusting the Lord to grant us safe travels.

April 26, 2011

The trip to Charleston went well and God granted us safe travels back home. Vera would not let Nita assist her at the rest stop. We got back to Millbrook in good time. It was a rollercoaster week. I must journal daily as I tend to miss events as they occur. Vera and I went to SPOLIWA Bible Camp to help with raking and clean-up on Tuesday. The plan was to spend the day and stay overnight. However, Vera would have none of that. She seemingly forgets and did not care about staying the night. So we returned home that evening. I was tired. I stayed in the guest room a few nights as she told me that the bedroom was off limits to me since I did not live here. I did not fuss and went to sleep in the guest room. She slept on the sofa. I would get a cover for her. The rest of the week was alright. Seemingly, anytime we go to church she gets a bit agitated when we arrive and is hesitant to go inside. I pray God will give victory in this area as the enemy does not want us to fellowship. However, whenever evening hits things seem to change. I learned from the dementia support group that evening time is difficult. We had Sunday dinner with some very dear friends, Aundrey and Nadine Wingate. We had a swell time of fun and laughter; I felt it was much needed. Monday morning came and I thank God for another day. Vera was mad at me for no reason, yet I thank God for His grace. I am praying daily for Vera's healing. She slept on the sofa again last night. This evening I managed to get her into the bed, and I am praying she and I will both have a good night sleep.

April 29, 2011

The last few days have been alright. I perceived some minor changes in Vera's perception. We still take walks daily and as often as we can. Seemingly night time is more of a challenge to get her to sleep in the bed. I noticed yesterday she seemingly is having problems with bladder control. I might be prudent to purchase some pads for her to use. I love my wife and will continue to do what I can for her. She is sitting across from me at the table; she just got through eating some butter pecan ice cream with strawberry topping. I was laid off last year and I see the hand of God in it all. He was in it after all and all the time. He allowed us to become debt-free so I could be at home to take care of Vera. I am so grateful to God. Vera and I have spent a lot of time together and I enjoy her company. Some days are more trying than others, but I am cherishing every moment we have together. To God be the glory!

May 4, 2011

Praise God for a great day. As we emerged from the weekend, I thank God for directing our week. There are times when Vera becomes agitated in the mornings. I have learned to wait it out, knowing that it's only temporary. God has been gracious unto us. Monday went well. We had a swell day; we did our bank and post office run and picked up a few graduation cards for the students. We had a quiet evening at home; we did our daily walk; I cut the grass; and I enjoyed the day with Vera. We slept soundly through the night. I got up for devotions, and when Vera arose it was a challenge as she blamed me for everything. I held back replying as it would fuel the situation more. Tuesday morning I'd planned to go to Birmingham Theological Seminary (BTS) for a presentation and I did not need the added stress of what was happening. Yet, I prayed to God to work on our behalf. Our son, David, was home and Nadine was coming over to spend a few hours with Vera while I was at BTS. I left around 9:35 AM and returned home around 2 PM. The presentation at BTS went well, and things at home were alright too. I thanked the Lord for guiding and sustaining us this day. We stayed in most of the afternoon. I took Vera for a drive to get out the house for a little while. God is so good. The night was swell as we slept. We got up, and there was a little complaining, but we ate breakfast together, went to the commissary, stopped by Affordable Eyewear, and returned home. We spent the afternoon together and went for our daily walk. We returned and ate dinner together. Then we prepared ourselves to go to Open Door Christian Faith Church to share marriage information. Vera allowed me to help her get dressed, and we had a swell time in fellowship with the saints. She did well sitting as I shared information with this congregation. We returned home, picked up a couple of Whoppers, and had a glass of lemonade. She finished with a cup of tea. I am about to get her out of the den, and hopefully she will go to bed for a good night sleep.

May 9, 2011

Thursday arrived. We had a swell day and enjoyed the evening at Bible study. Friday was more of the same as we spent more time together. I was concerned about my continuing to serve on an Allied Health Board. I spoke with Patrick, one of my sons, and Nate Brock, a very dear Brother in Christ, regarding staying on the American Medical Technologists Board of Directors. They both recommended I remain on the board as long as I can. It will give me an outlet. I will look further into bringing home health support at least 4 hours a week so Vera can get use to someone else, and it will give me a few hours to do something for myself. I love my wife, but as her primary caregiver I too must keep myself in good shape. We still have moments of ups and downs when she goes through some changes. I am learning to be patient and wait. Sometimes she still kicks me out of the bedroom so I sleep in the guest bedroom.

Saturday was eventful. We had a blessed morning, went to the commissary, and gave out a few fliers on marriage. Nighttime came quickly. Vera strolled around all evening. We got up in the morning and prepared to get ready for church. As we arrived at Sanctuary Vera still gets a bit agitated and hesitant to go inside. I thank God for the support of church family. We had a blessed day. I was asked to bring the morning message. Nita and Sam came by and we ate dinner together. I'm so glad they live near us. We had a good evening with lots of laughter and fun for a change. Night came along. I managed to get Vera into the bed. I chose to sleep in the guest room because Vera said I was no longer her husband and to stay out of her room. As the Lord allowed us to see Monday morning, Vera awakened in a fussing mood. I said to myself, be patient and wait. After breakfast, I told her I needed her to accompany me to the church mother's home to mow her yard. After lunch, I persuaded her to take a shower and she did. We spent the rest of the day in the house. We ran a few errands in the evening and returned home. Now it is bed time, and I got to get her to go to bed. Lord help!

May 15, 2011

The week was rather eventful. I am taking one day at a time. We had an interesting day on Tuesday. We went to the commissary and spent the better part of the day preparing for a marriage retreat. We had a pleasant night. Wednesday was busy as we prepared for the marriage seminar. Vera was very helpful. We had a blessed time at Open Door Christian Faith Church. The church prayed for us in preparation for our trip to Charleston. Their prayers of intercession was much needed and welcomed! We had a restful night, and Vera was very much in tuned as we made an early departure for Charleston. The Lord gave us safe travels. We got to visit with my mother, and we attend Memorial Baptist Church with

Vera's sister, Joy, and husband, Joe. Vera did quite well. We sat in the back of the church as she did not want to go further. The services went well. Night was a little challenging. Vera slept in the room adjacent mine. Morning arrived. I assisted her with bathroom duties, and she became very upset. She yelled at me and refused to accept my help. I waited for a while, and she was more accommodating. Thank God! The day went well as we visited with family. We returned and spent the rest of the day at the house. I looked over some notes in preparation for Sunday services. We had a good night sleep; as I attempted to dress Vera she started fussing at her reflection in the mirror and was quite abusive to me as well. She finally calmed down as we left for Sumter. We had a very good conference at New Life Bible Church and returned to Charleston late that afternoon. After a brief rest period we visited with my brother and his wife for several hours and returned back to the house. We made preparation for bed; she finally crawled into the bed. We had a good time getting dressed for morning services. She did well at Holy Trinity AME Church. My sister-in-law, Delphine, sat with her during services. After services at Holy Trinity, the Lord blessed us with safe travels back to Millbrook. Vera is now in bed, and I am about to turn in too. Thank God! God is faithful, and I thank Him for a blessed weekend trip together.

May 18, 2011

Praise God for a good day. Things went very well today. Vera awakened early this morning, and I was sleeping at the foot of the bed since she had fallen asleep and taken up most of the bed. She was a bit disoriented, yet the day unfolded in a nice way. We spent most of the day together. We prepared to complete our last session with Open Door Christian Faith Church. The evening session went swell. We thank God for the opportunity to share with this congregation. It is time to turn in for the night. Vera is already in the bed and I am off in that direction too. David is about to head off to work for the night. Thank you, God, for your grace.

May 25, 2011

Sunday started off a bit rough, but we went on to Sunday school and morning services. Vera did well, and we returned home. We spent the rest of the day at home. Monday went well. We did a few things around the house with Vera's assistance. I am making a good attempt to enjoy each day we have. I thank God daily for His grace. Some days are a bit more trying than others especially when she forgets who I am. I try to hold on and get through the storm of accusations which this disease process has caused and pray again and daily for God's restoring her. She slept on the sofa most of the night. Sometimes if I wait long enough she'll get up at my bidding and go to bed. Tuesday was more of the same. She went with me to the commissary as we do on Tuesday mornings. We met some dear friends, Freddie and Betty Prince, there and talked for a bit. I also spoke with Pastor Cromblin who wants us to return to his church and share more information with his congregation on marriage and resolving conflicts. I thank

God for this upcoming opportunity. We returned home and spent most of the day around the house.

We went walking late morning and as always enjoyed the walks together. Tuesday night I allowed Vera to sleep in bed by herself, and I returned to the guest room. I was having devotions when Vera came into the room. She left and returned and I noticed she needed help having to change her undergarments. After helping her, the morning was a challenge as she seemed very agitated. I kept my distance for a while and sought to speak very little. She ate breakfast, and we shared lunch. Now she is napping next to me on the couch in the den. I do pray the rest of the day goes well. I will be going to pick up the shipment of the books tonight. She'll accompany me to pick them up. Lord, please help my wife and grant her a restful rest of the day. She needs your healing touch, and I will pray daily for your healing and restoration for her.

May 28, 2011

Reflecting over the past few days has been challenging as I see a little more decline in Vera. I still try to communicate with my love throughout the day and to engage her in conversation. She naps more than before. I am still asking the Lord to restore and heal my wife. This morning I was encouraged during my quiet time that "God is always in control." Even during our painful moments He is still in control and can use it for our good. Vera accompanied me downtown on several trips. Most of the chores are caught up around the house so we find ourselves relaxing in the den. There are times we have a great time sharing. Then there are times she is very agitated. It is during those times I must smile and bear. God, you know what I am enduring. I ask daily for your grace. It's hard to see one's mate slowly decline. She needs my help and at times fights me because to her I have done some things wrong. It takes a while for her to get over this. I love her with all my heart and will continue to do so. I will pour more love on her. Even now my heart is heavy as I ask her to allow me to set her hair in preparation for church services tomorrow. I trust the rest of our day will be restful and enjoyable! I am counting it all joy.

June 20, 2011

Praise the Lord. We had a great week at camp. Vera did quite well, and now we are home. We are getting back into our routine and trusting the Lord to continue to meet needs. I came down with a head and chest cold this weekend. This morning I am still trying to kick it! It seems it's more difficult tending to Vera and still trying to take care of myself. Lord, I need your help today. We are about to go to the bank, but before that I think we'll have a moment to reflect on the Word of God. I praise God for this day. I have a decision to make soon regarding my continuing with the American Medical Technologists (AMT) Board of Directors. I am praying for wisdom and guidance as I am required to spend several weekends away from home, and I am concerned about

Vera's care. Lord, I pray for wisdom and direction regarding this decision.

June 22, 2011

Monday night was tough as Vera went through a very difficult time. She was accusing me; I felt so helpless, and it took everything within me to pray and be patient. Every time she falls asleep on the sofa in the den, it takes a lot to get her to respond and go to bed. So she stayed in the den. I went to bed, and when she came into the room early that morning, she began fussing. I pray to God during those times more so for understanding and patience. The next day we attended a leadership meeting at our church, and she did well with that. Praise God we had a good night's sleep, yet Wednesday morning it was just a little more of the same. I try helping and am accused. So I resolved to take it slow. Lord, You know what we need, and I pray for grace and strength for this day! The remainder of the day went well.

July 1, 2011

My, the week has flown by. The Lord blessed us with a powerful youth and scholarship day service at church. Since Sunday, Vera and I had been having a great week. The evenings have been busy with VBS attendance. We attended Bible study last night and were encouraged. Throughout the week we spent time in devotion and prayer together. I thank God for those moments as we shared with each other. Her thoughts seem to go from one thing to another, yet I am thankful we have a dialogue and are sharing with each other. She assisted me in visiting with church members, Darryl and Ruby Smith, taking food and communing together. I am grateful for my mate and thank God for each day He gives us to share together. This morning I have completed our monthly finances. Carmela, my older daughter, consented to come down to Miami during the AMT national convention for 3-4 days. She will be able to spend time with Vera while I'm busy on Friday and Saturday with board business. Thank God for providing the funds to assist Mel in making the trip. I rejoiced in the God of our salvation and pray that He will continue ordering our steps day by day.

July 4, 2011

The weekend went swell. We attended Sunday school and morning services, and Vera did well at both services. I thank God for my church sister, Pamela Brown, who normally sits with Vera and helps her during services. Early Monday morning Vera got up, and I was awakened and inquired if she needed assistance using the restroom. She told me that she did not ask me for help. So I proceeded to go to the guest room since she also stated that the bed was hers. Lord, this is so difficult hearing that, but I give it all to you. Ease my hurt and enable me to minister to my wife. Morning arriving, she would come in and out of the guest room. I had my devotions, prayed, and then asked if she needed anything. She allowed me to help her with bathing and getting dressed. The day went just fine. We ate breakfast together. I proceeded to cook dinner for the day, barbecuing and fixing some other goodies. Overall, the day went well. Night came quickly. I helped her get her night clothes on. She's in bed now. I am finishing a few items and will turn in also. I thank God for a good day.

August 9, 2011

The weekend came quickly and we were off to Atlanta on Sunday morning for a flight to Miami for the AMT national convention. Overall, we had a great week. I think Vera did swell considering being in an unfamiliar setting. She did alright at all social functions. Wednesday night she was hesitant to leave after the OGM-MOM dinner. The awards banquet and the Friday night social went quite well. Early in the week we spent quite a bit of time together. David looked out for his Mom when I needed to be gone. Mel arrived Thursday and stood in the gap for the remainder of the week. Vera still was a bit agitated when Mel arrived,; sometimes becoming rather verbally abusive,; yet, we realized that God is still in control. Vera got a bit sick Saturday night, probably from something she ate earlier. We gave her ginger ale and crackers along with a Tum that seem to settle her stomach. My sister, Delores, brother-in-law, Nat, and my niece, Karen, came by for a visit Saturday evening. It was a joy to see them again. We got up early Sunday morning and took a cab to the airport. The flight back to Atlanta was quick and when time to de-board Vera did not want to get off the plane. But she finally conceded. We retrieved our luggage, got the van, and the Lord gave us safe travel back to Millbrook. We were rather tired from the week long events and rested for the remainder of the day. Lord, I thank you for taking care of us during the week. Vera and I had several moments to reflect during a devotional time. I thank God for His grace and mercy. Lord, I thank you for granting us patience. Today, I am grateful that she is having a good day. She is taking a nap now, and I will ask her to help with dinner preparations when she awakens. Thank you Lord for everything!

This has been a good week. Vera is becoming quieter. She tends to nap more. I have to get her more involved in doing something to keep her interest afresh. Sometimes she looks at me like she doesn't know me. Then there are times she calls me by my name. I want to enjoy each day God gives us. We have been busy around the house. Trying to keep things in order. It's good to be back to our routine and making our rounds in Millbrook and Prattville. She accompanied me to the grocery store on Tuesday. I noticed that she will speak to anyone who comes along. I must keep an eye on her as she has a tendency to go another way. I call out to her by name, and she returns. I guess I have become a bit over-protective, but I want to ensure that all is well for her. I do have time for myself. David may keep an eye on Vera so I can get away for a while. This week she has allowed me to help her without problems: restroom, showers, getting dress, etc. We had a great time at Bible study. Afterwards, she went into the sanctuary and enjoyed the music the choir was rehearsing. God has kept her. I pray daily for her recovery and deliverance. I know God is able to heal and restore her. Lord, whatever your purpose is for this affliction, still I will trust you. Today she did swell as she helped me repair the riding lawnmower. I finished mowing the backyard. Afterwards, we went to take care of church Mother Averhart's yard. She enjoyed the visit with mother. We left, got gas, bought lunch and came home and ate lunch together. Overall, it was a good day. We had a great time listening to some old tunes from the 60's. It brought back a lot of memories. Night time came quickly. She is asleep now. I have been reflecting over Scripture as to what to share on Sunday morning and praying for God's direction. I am about to turn in now. She told me earlier, I'd better sleep in my own bed. Oh, well! Thank you Lord! I will sneak into the same bed and pray for a restful night.

August 17, 2011

This morning started with a bang, and I retreated to wait things out. My earlier devotion covered the topic "being patient." The Lord prepared me for the outburst at 5:30 AM. I went to help Vera with some personal issues and was verbally blasted. So I waited until a more favorable time; I needed to assist her and went ahead anyway and took more abuse. Yes, I love her and it did weigh on me considerably, yet, I thank God for my wife who I love dearly. As the day progressed I stayed quiet and allowed her some space. I went outside early to do yard work. She would come to the door and watch me. She did come outside and I asked for her help.

August 20, 2011

Well, it's Saturday morning. The rest of the week went rather well. Bible study went real well; we accomplished things around the house, mainly cleaning up the yard (front and back). God is teaching me patience through the affliction that my wife is enduring. Vera and I took a drive to Wetumpka yesterday afternoon to locate a church which will be purchasing some books from us for their bible college. Last night she went to sleep on the sofa. I knew I was in for trouble. She awoke early this morning. I went to assist her in using the restroom; she refused and came back later to use the restroom without completely disrobing. I went to help and was verbally abused. Sometimes she would hit me claiming that I hurt the children or had done something to her mother. I reflected on Psalm 73:24: "He will guide me through his counsel, and afterward receive me unto glory." I tried successfully in giving her a shower. She was still aggravated with me. I think at times she does not know me as her husband. This is also difficult for me, but I continue to be quiet and when available I assist her. This occurred around 4:30 AM. Now it is 10 AM, and she has become more cordial. We took a trip to the post office and returned home. I pray the rest of the day goes well. I thank you, Lord, for your help and strength. Please continue to bring healing to my wife. I commit this day unto You, Oh Lord. I determine not to give the enemy any ground. I praise God for the victory that is already ours! I was encouraged in this morning's devotion regarding being a servant. I trust to be a servant of the Most High God!

August 22, 2011

We went to Sanctuary on yesterday morning. She was very hesitant about going inside and wanted to go back home, supposing she had a lot of things to do. Pastor McKenzie approached the door and encouraged her to come inside which she did. Sunday school and morning services went well, and she did fine. We returned home. I prepared okra soup and rice, and we enjoyed the rest of the day at home. I encouraged her to go with me to Dairy Queen. We went and enjoyed a sundae and blizzard. I spent a few moments reading the 36 hour day book regarding dementia. I found out that towards the evening the loved one has a tendency to become more aggravated. As we prepared for bed, she went to sleep on the sofa. I waited until later and finally encouraged her to come to bed which she did. She got up early and I found her on the sofa again, to which I brought her back to bed. I got up and invited her to go walking with me, but she refused; so I went for a 30-minute walk around the neighborhood. I am trying to get back into walking at least 4-5 times a week for 30 minutes. Lord knows I need the exercise. When I walk alone it affords me time to pray and reflect. I need to find some other things for Vera and me to do during the day, maybe volunteering, etc. I know Vera's limited in what she can do, but I feel keeping her a little busy will help her feel productive. This disease is terminal in that there is no cure. The meds she's taking do provide some relief. I pray daily for God's healing virtue and restoration of my wife. She just told me that she would like to go fishing. It would be a good outing for both of us. We had devotion this morning, but I perceive that she was not very receptive to the reading. I pray daily for Vera to get better and ONLY Almighty God can bring about healing for her. Lord, I still thank and praise You for Your grace.

August 24, 2011

Today has been an unpleasant day. From the time Vera got up she has been very abusive verbally; nothing I do seems to satisfy. She is having increased problems using the restroom, urinating on the floor and not sitting on the commode. This is really a tough time for me as I try to help her. I am accused of doing everything wrong: I am called a liar; I hurt the children; I am not her husband. I need to go to my own house and leave her alone. She says, "I do not need your help!" I do not know how this night will finish out but I am mentally tired, and at times I feel that God should just end this ordeal. I was encouraged by a couple of cards I received from friends who wish me God's care; one in particular had lost her husband to Alzheimer's just a couple of weeks ago. Lord, I do not know how much more I can take. I realized that it is the disease process, but it is so overbearing. Lord, I pray you will give both of us a good night sleep. Yesterday evening at church, Vera sat there for nearly an hour and half as Pastor Brown, church member Renee Butler, and I discussed church business. We came home after stopping and getting a deli meal, then, we went to bed.

August 27, 2011

It's Saturday, and we are pressing on. Each day bring on new challenges. I am reminded that "all things work together for good, to those who love the Lord; to those who are called according to God's purpose" (Romans 8:28). I am to "give thanks in everything for this is the will of God in Christ Jesus concerning me" (I Thess. 5:17). It is very hard to view it in that light when things are going awry, when your mate has a degenerative disease and there is nothing you can do except to pray. God, I know you are aware of everything that pertains to Vera and me. I ask You to minister Your healing virtue to her as only You can. I will continue to trust in Your grace. I perceive shifts in her behavior. Sometimes she doesn't recognize me! "I feel like going on! Though trials come on every hand, I feel like going on!" Lord, still I will trust You. I hope the remainder of today goes well. The annual Mission Day Program will take place at church tomorrow. It's been a challenge getting her inside the church on Sundays and Thursday nights. I pray tomorrow will go well. I thank you God in advance for your divine grace and mercy.

August 29, 2011

It was a bit tough getting started Sunday morning. But, I was determined not to let the enemy have the upper hand. Vera would not let me help her get dressed and became rather volatile. I was very upset because I did nothing to aggravate her. Yet, I prayed and asked the Lord to give us strength. I prayed for both of us. After a while, she allowed me to help her get dressed. We left in time for church, and as we approached church Vera became a bit disturbed. However, after having entered and getting into the lesson she did well. We enjoyed the Sunday school and worship service. I helped her take care of personal needs after service. We had fellowship with the others after morning service. The afternoon program ensued, and Vera did great. I thank God for giving us victory on this day. We returned home, and ate the carry-out plate from church. We later turned in for the night, and God blessed our sleep. We got up this morning. I assisted her in the bathroom, fixed breakfast for us, and went to take the car for servicing while she stayed at home with David. As of now, the morning went well. We shared lunch together. The evening went well. She has retired to bed now, and I will go to bed shortly myself. Lord, You have been good to us, and I am grateful for a blessed day. I have almost completed the Sunday school conference flier. I received a call from Annette Thompson inviting me to speak for Pastor Johnson's appreciation service on October 2, 2011. I am looking forward to fellowship with our friends at New Life Bible Church. Lord, I pray you will give Vera and me a good night sleep. I am praying also that David will have a good night at work.

September 5, 2011

Lord, I pause to thank you for your many blessings towards us. I had the pleasure of attending the caregivers support group at Fraser last Thursday, and it was encouraging. I hope to continue attending. David sat with his Mom while I went; I needed that time away. Upon my return home Vera was looking for me. We have gotten so use to being together. Then there are times when the disease affects her memory and I am not Paul, especially when she awakes in the morning. I have trouble getting her to use the toilet and that escalates into more problems. But, I must continue to be there for her regardless of what's happening. I have to pick my battles. She went to lunch with me on last Friday in celebration of my birthday. Saturday was eventful. We had a good morning. She, David, and I went to visit with Nita and Sam; we had a great time, a very tasty dinner and it was just good getting time away. We returned home and got settled in for the night. David went to work, and Vera fell asleep. She crawled upon the bed on top of the cover, so I covered her up, and she slept that way all night. I got myself a blanket and went to sleep.

Sunday morning started a bit rough as she would not let me assist her, and she started accusing me again; I was really tired of the accusations. I went to the living room to take a break. Then I got up to getting back with her. She, with much hesitation, allowed me to finish helping her get dressed. We went to church and had a blessed time in Sunday school and morning worship. We returned home and was blessed to eat dinner together. The remainder of the day was quiet. Church member, Jeanette McKinzie, came by and shared a video with us, and I had a good time conferring with her. Later that evening I helped Vera get ready for bed. I came to bed later. She awoke earlier in the morning and had trouble getting to the restroom and would not allow me to help her. Needless to say I had to clean up the floor and her as well. I was so frustrated I went to bed in the guest room. She was up most of the early morning. She never went back to sleep. She urinated on the floor in the restroom again and I had to mop it up. I managed to clean her up with a birdie bath because she refused to take a shower. I am learning to pick my battles. Today went well. Now it's time to turn in again. I hope to get her to bed and pray she'll sleep through the entire night.

September 7, 2011

I spent Monday night in the guest room again because she told me I could not sleep in her bedroom. Again, I resorted not to fuss. She did not sleep the entire night and was up most of the early morning. Upon awakening, she did allow me to help her take a shower. Of course the conversation at every shower is that I did something wrong and that she is not going to stay here any longer. I continue to pray for strength daily. After the shower, I prepared breakfast for us. I am thankful that Vera has a good appetite; I called David and asked him to bring some milk; he forgot. So I prepared grits, mustard sardines, toast, eggs, coffee and juice for us. She ate it all! I asked her to go with me to the commissary; she agreed. We stopped by Millbrook Printers to drop of the newsletter for copy service. We went to the grocery store. She seemed to talk to a lot of people while at the store. She enjoyed being out, and I plan to get her out of the house often. We purchased a couple of chicken sandwiches. We stopped by WVAS to pick up a few CD's I won on the radio and then returned home. After having put away the groceries, we shared lunch together. The remainder of the day was quietly spent at home. The rest of the day went well, and we had a good time together at home. We were blessed to sleep in the same bed as she was tired and slept the entire night through, thanks be unto God. This morning I arose and had my quiet time. Then I began to prepare some pancake breakfast; she awoke. I finished everything except the eggs. I assisted her with showers and got her dressed, came back and completed the eggs, and we had a good breakfast together. I shared a devotional with her. We left for a shoe store to get a few shoe boxes for Samaritan Purse, dropped by Walmart to check on some pants for David, and went to The Dollar Tree to purchase items for the shoe box. Then we stopped by Lowes to purchase a package of bulbs and returned home. She is beside me now enjoying a bowl of juicy oranges. The days seem to be coming along alright. Night has arrived; I pray we'll have a good night sleep.

September 29, 2011

The past few days have been alright. A couple of nights I resorted to sleep in the guest room and den to avoid problems. This morning I got up a bit early to help Vera change her pajamas; needless to say that was a real challenge. I proceeded to help her in the shower and assisted her in getting dressed. I likewise did the same. We had breakfast and devotion. I am spending some time today reviewing for

Bible class this evening and reflecting on what to share for Sunday with the New Life family. I wanted to take her out to lunch at Shoney's. Upon arriving she changed her mind. She needs more assistance each day and still is adamant that she doesn't need my help. It's hard for me when she tells me that I should go to my own house. She has a tendency to stand at the front door and peer outside. Occasionally she will talk to the mirror and on occasion fuss with her reflection in the mirror. I would take her with me most times to the stores, post office, bank, and recycle in order to get out the house for a while. We would walk sometimes which tends to be a good thing. I am about to fix some lunch for us and then I will spend more time reviewing notes. Lord, I thank you for all your help and grace. It's hard watching her decline ever so slowly. But, I am still going to commit my requests to Almighty God who is able to heal and restore.

October 8, 2011

Thank the Lord for Saturday morning. We made an attempt to go to Prattville to see little DJ play soccer. We arrived at the park, but Vera changed her mind and wanted to return home. We came back home, and I proceeded to wash two cars. I also took some time to start cleaning out the shed. This was my action plan for the week. I plan to spend at least 1 hour per week until the shed is cleaned and unused junk thrown out! I asked her to go with me to the church leadership meeting this afternoon. I trust things will go well with that trip.

The leadership meeting went well and Vera did fine in attending. We returned home, picked up a meal from the deli and stayed in the rest of the night. Vera is in bed now, and I am about to turn in. I am praying for a good night sleep. We awakened by God's grace and had a blessed day of worship at Sanctuary. We were surprised and blessed as Renita and Sam came to worship with us. Renita danced to the glory of God. Vera was so elated during the dance that she praised God for Renita: "That's my daughter; she's a woman of God!" Pastor Brown encouraged us through the word! We came home. Renita prepared the meal; we had a great time of fellowship. We remained home for the rest of the day. I thank God for His grace towards us. Vera is doing very well today. I have been reminding her that I will be gone for 2 days and that Renita will come and stay with her. I pray that things will go well. Vera and I took a ride to Marbury to find Union Baptist Church. We had a swell trip on such a lovely fall day.

October 15, 2011

I returned home this evening from Chicago. Renita did a great job caring for her Mom. Vera did ok up until Friday night. However, she ate when I came home, took a shower, and now she's sleeping. I pray she'll sleep the whole night through. Lord willing, we'll look forward to a great day tomorrow. I miss her so much, and it's good to be home again. I am praying God to meet her every need. I thank you, God, for safe travel and watching over my family.

October 20, 2011

The Lord woke us up this morning. Vera got up a bit early. I stayed in bed for another hour or two. Then I went and got her, and we took showers. I got her dressed, and we ate breakfast and had devotions together. I am thankful in that the day appears to be another good one. Home health arrived, and I left for class. I had a good day in the class and returned home. Vera seems to have done alright with the home health nurse. I spoke with the nurse at length until her ride came. Afterwards, Vera and I had lunch together. I spent some time completing some inspection forms, and we rested in the den watching TV for a while. We were blessed from our time at Bible study. We returned home to a pizza David had prepared for us. Vera has just turned in for the night. I am looking forward to a good night sleep.

October 28, 2011

Thursday morning came, and we thank God for waking us up. Vera and I had breakfast and devotion. Ms. Elaine, the home health nurse, arrived and I went on to my weekly class. It was quite refreshing driving up to Tallassee as it granted me an opportunity to pray and reflect. After class was over, I returned home by way of Highway 14; it was a gorgeous day to drive along the country highway. God is so good. I arrived home safely, and all was well. I thanked Elaine for her services and gave her a piece of carrot cake too. Vera and I went and got a deli meal for lunch. I prepared a handout for Bible class. We had a blessed time at Bible study. We returned home, and ate a small portion of chicken, squash and rice. Vera was ready for bed. She fell asleep on the sofa. I managed to get her to bed. She took up most of the bed. I came later and slept at the foot of the bed. Thank God for a good night sleep. Vera got up early this morning. I assisted her with the restroom and she returned back to bed. I got up later on and went to have my quiet time. She got up later and came in the guest room where I was. We went to the shower and got cleaned up. We got dressed and left for the commissary, gas station, bank and hospital lab. I saw a friend who bought a book, and one of her friends bought a book too. Lord, I thank you for favor. We came home and brought the groceries in the house. Soon thereafter I made lunch for us. I spent part of the afternoon mowing the back yard and cleaning the den. The rest of the day went well. I see where it is taking Vera longer to understand basic instructions to do things. She tends to stand around in one spot, whispering, staring, just being quiet. She tends to nap more frequently. I am trying to keep her up since it's only 7:25 PM. I hope I can keep her awake until about 9-9:30PM.

October 29, 2011

Well, she got up near midnight and probably did not go back to sleep. I was in the guest room last evening, and she came in complaining. I tried to get her to bed to no avail. She did allow me to help her put on her night clothes. I feel helpless as she talks out of her head about things, accusing me of taking her things, hurting the children and bothering stuff in her house. I was told to get out. This talking rolled on until this morning. I helped her shower and fixed breakfast for us. I changed her clothes and fixed her hair and face. As I look at my wife I cry inside. Lord, what more can I do? She keeps saying this is mine. I am going to take her out with me this morning to make a few rounds. I pray God will touch her mind and bring healing and restoration in the mighty Name of Jesus! In the Name of Jesus I rebuke the enemy! In the Name of Jesus I pray for my wife. Lord, I commit this day to You. Your will be done today in our lives. The day went well. We spent most of the time in the house. We went to a friend to get a table. Vera accompanied me to Office Depot, and we returned home. We watched football for a while and ate dinner. I rolled her hair and took out clothes for her to wear to church in the morning. I pray we'll have a better night tonight. I will try to keep her up if possible a little late so she'll sleep through the night.

November 4, 2011

Sunday morning came and I thank God that we arose and got ready for church. We ate breakfast and went to Sunday school and morning worship. Everything thing went well. Vera helped me sing a closing song in Sunday school. We had a very encouraging service. We returned home and had dinner I then went to Rebirth Christian Ministries for a book signing. The service there went well, and I was blessed to sell a few books. I made contact for a future marriage workshop. I thank God for this open door. Sunday night all went well. The week went well as Vera help me with various chores around the house. The nights have been alright. I spent most of this week in our bedroom. Vera has a tendency to get up early in the morning and walk around until I get up. We would have breakfast together. I look forward to those times in the morning, and we also share devotions. I would read and she would comment on the topic at hand. I attended the fifth class in Tallassee. Elaine Parks came over again to sit with Vera. That seems to be going well. I have one more class to attend. I am praying about using Elaine's services after the class has ended. Vera seems to have taken a liking to Ms. Parks. I am thankful to God that things are as well as they are. God has been good to us. Even though she is going through this affliction of dementia, I am still praying for God to heal her. I am enjoying spending time with her. Some days are a challenge, but for the most part this past week has been a real blessing. It's difficult when she does not remember me. I cry within myself as we sit at the table and I ask her to do a task and she cannot and doesn't seem to fully understand. It's then that I help her through the process. She is wearing Depends now. Most times when we go out I ensure she wears one. I also ask her to use the restroom before we leave the house. I will, throughout the day, ask her if she needs to use the restroom. She has been agreeable.

Vera was most hesitant about staying for Bible study. Pam came and got her out of the hallway. She did well at study. We returned home and ate a pizza. The Lord gave us a good night sleep. Vera awoke early as usual. I stayed as long as I could in bed and then got up. I assisted her with a shower and fixed pancakes for us. We had a good time at the table and shared devotion. We got dressed, and she went with me on a few errands. We enjoyed turkey burgers and fries for lunch. I took care of a few communications on the computer. I relaxed with her in the den. Then I went back to make a bank deposit and now updating the diary. I thank God for a good day and pray the evening will be just as well. I must spend some time preparing a message for Sunday services. Lord, I thank You for this season and pray daily for grace and strength to accomplish whatever You have for me.

November 10, 2011

Last night I was kicked out of the room. So I went to the guest room and slept. Vera went to sleep and again got up early and stayed up most of the morning. She was very irritated. I can't put my finger on anything specific that irritated her, yet I kept to myself. She allowed me to help her shower and get dressed. We ate breakfast together. Elaine Parks came over and stayed with her while I went to my final class. The class has been very helpful, allowing me to employ some principles of living well and managing my wife's illness in the best possible way. The rest of the day went well. We had a very informative and blessed time at Bible study. We picked up a deli meal and returned home. After eating, I helped Vera get her pajamas on and prepared her a cup of tea. She is now about ready for bed and so am I. Praying we'll have a good night sleep. Lord, I thank you for this day that you have ordained. I pray your will to be done in and through our lives. Thanks for a blessed day.

November 13, 2011

The weekend has been quite enjoyable. We spent Friday around the house that morning. David drove us to Renita and Sam's house to get him acquainted with directions to their house. We returned and had a quiet evening at home. Saturday Mel came and spent the day; we enjoyed her visit. Nita stopped by later to spend time with Mel. Mom seems a bit agitated, yet the girls understand what's happening and were able to continue encouraging Mom. Mel stayed the night and got up early to leave. I fixed breakfast for the three of us. As she went to get the rest of her things, I continued encouraging Vera to eat breakfast. It's really hard seeing her decline in this way. My eyes watered up when Mel left the kitchen as I tended to Vera. I do not know what else to do. I pray daily for her recovery and ask the Lord to bring healing and restoration for her. I will continue to daily intercede on her behalf. I know the Lord is aware of our season, and I pray for grace for each day. It's Sunday evening and we are watching football. Vera is napping in the den. We will be preparing for our trip to Pat and Cherrie's. I pray even now that the days spent there will be restful and joyous. Lord, I thank you for this day and that things are as well as they are!

November 21, 2011

We had a good trip to Columbus and the Lord protected us during our travels. We arrived at Pat and Cherrie's around 4:30 PM. One of my granddaughters, Aisha, was waiting on us and we have been very busy entertaining her these past few days. We rested very well Thursday night. We spent most of Friday around the house, enjoying being with the grandkids and spending time with Cherrie and Pat. Vera has been very agitated being in these surroundings. She has been very vocal and really bothered. I perceive with her being out-of-place and in this different environment, it hasn't settled well at all. The kids have been briefed on the changes that their grandma is experiencing. I pray they understand.

The marriage workshop went well. We had three couples in attendance. Vera was rather edgy, but we continued the presentation. She shared some things during the workshop. Sunday morning was a challenge. During our time at church she was again a bit vocal. I prayed for her to have the peace of God. Mother Bell sat with her during the time I shared the word; I am thankful for the prayer support of the saints. I pray that the rest of our time here will be enjoyable for the both of us. Mel and family, David, Nita and Sam are due to arrive on Wednesday. I trust Vera will be acceptable of their presence. I pray God will grant us a great rest of the week. She accompanied me to the store to purchase a dishwasher for Pat and Cherrie, an early Christmas gift as they needed one. We stopped by Walmart to pick up a few items and returned back to the house.

November 28, 2011

The rest of the stay at Pat and Cherrie's went alright. Vera was still agitated; I suppose being displaced for 9 days was a bit taxing. I have resolved to limit anymore overnight stays, especially of that duration. She interacted with everyone, and I thank God for her being with me. The family has accepted her affliction and is praying for her healing and restoration. Thanksgiving Day was a blessing, sitting around the table, laughing, praying, and encouraging each other was a joy. Vera sat at the table after some coaxing and the time was enjoyable. We'd plan to leave Friday morning and decided to stay until Saturday. I got some special time to chat with Patrick and really appreciated him for taking the time to share with me. I was able to help him take care of a few maintenance items around the house. Mel and the family left early Saturday morning. Vera and I left at 6:05 AM. Nita, Sam and David left a few hours later. The Lord gave us all safe travel back home. Vera was very anxious when it was time for her and me to leave. We stopped for breakfast at a drive-thru and continued on. We stopped at the Tennessee welcome center, but she refused to use the restroom. We continued and stopped for gas and a Chi Fila for lunch. We arrived at home around 3:50 PM. I thank God for safety on the roads. Since arriving home Saturday evening, it has taken her a while to get readjusted. She continues to talk to the mirrors or seemingly as if someone is standing by. Of course I have been accused of wrongdoing, and I try to keep a distance until needed. I am praying daily for her recovery if the Lord wills. There were times I did ask the Lord to not allow her to suffer so, yet I am reminded that God said, "My grace is sufficient for thee." I pray to stay close to my wife and serve her daily. I am praying for approval of support from the Central Alabama Aging Consortium. We will have a visit from Jane Mitchel on Friday morning to assess services that Vera may qualify for. I pray she'll get the services and voucher approval.

Vera just came into the kitchen. She has a tendency to shake her hands more often. I feel at a loss as to how I could help her. We plan to decorate the house for Christmas today. It will allow us time to spend together. My eyes tear up as I observed her in this state and can do nothing but pray and be available to help and serve her when needed. Lord, you are aware of our plight, and I call upon you this morning for help and your presence. We took a little time this morning to run a few errands. We plan to set up a booth in the Village Green Park during the Christmas parade in hopes of selling some books and maybe some carrot cakes, possibly may get some orders. Lord, I commit this day back to you. Thanks for being our great God and Savior.

December 1, 2011

Wednesday came, and we had a reasonably good day. Vera is still acclimating to being home. I do not think we will be doing any more extended days away from home, which is her familiar territory. I was kicked out of the bedroom last night, yet she did not sleep in the bedroom. I think she was up most of the night. Tuesday night she slept on the sofa in the den all night. I try to help her any time I can or when she will allow me to. This morning we got under way. We spent the morning together. I left for my monthly support group session and returned to have lunch together. Jane Mitchel came over to assess needs and will be sending some vouchers we can use for respite services. Thank God for this assistance. We ate dinner together; she has a good appetite. We left for Bible study and had a good study. Vera went off to sleep, being very tired. We returned home and had a little something light. She went to bed now. I hope to join her shortly. I pray we both will sleep the entire night through. Thank God for another good day!

December 20, 2011

I am getting very tired. After a good day, it seems when night approaches things always go downhill. We had a good day today. We went to the store, stopped to get blood drawn, returned home and had lunch, and spent the rest of the day relaxing, talking, and resting. We had a good dinner together. Now that night time is here, and I try to get Vera to put on her night clothes, it just escalates and it's very tiring for me. I will sleep in the guest room from now on. She may or may not sleep in our bedroom, but I am tired of the drama. I will avail myself to assist when needed, but I am going to keep my distance. Lord, only you know what the end holds. This disease is very destructive physically, emotionally, and in other ways. I love Vera more than words can say, but the dementia is getting to me, Lord, and I need your power and guidance to minister to my wife. I cannot do this on my own. I definitely will not be going to Charleston this week and for a while. I have a ministry board meeting coming up next month, and I may ask Renita to come down and stay with her Mom while I go to Georgia. Lord, I need your direction and guidance. I need your help. I cannot do this on my own. I can keep up with everything else, but the shouting, accusing, hitting, biting, cursing, is not my wife but the disease. I am pleading if you would heal her from this dreadful disease and bring restoration to her mind and body. I can only hope for a good night sleep this evening.

December 22, 2011

Yesterday went reasonably well. The weather was damp, drizzling in and out. Vera and I did take a walk when the sun came out for a while. I reflect on the importance of living life to the fullest, even if allowed to get old, we can still make a difference for God. I was very upset yesterday, but thank God for this journey. He is still in control of my life and will use this season for good. I tried last night to get Vera to sleep in the bed to no avail. So I covered her up on the den sofa and went to bed. She got up at some point during the morning and stayed up. I tried several times to get her to come to bed, but she did not. I did not want to aggravate her so I left it alone. I took a shower and had devotions. After praying for her, I asked the Lord to give her peace and prayed she would accept my help. She did take a shower and allowed me to help her get dressed. She ate a hearty breakfast of pancakes. Now she is asleep on the den sofa. I covered her and hope she'll stay there a while. God, you are good and your mercies endure forever. I plan to review my notes for Bible study tonight. If she desires to go I will take her or if not I may leave her with David. I pray God will speak to Vera's heart, give her peace, and bring total healing to her body. I pray for us to continue working together, presenting valuable insight to couples when the opportunity avails itself. Lord, I commit this day back to you.

December 28, 2011

Tuesday morning was good. The weather was cloudy and cold. Thus we stayed inside most of the day. The day was rather relaxing. I got quite a bit done around the house. As evening approached I notice Vera was a bit agitated. She was good the whole time family was here. Now it's back to accusations. I am determined to not let it get the best of me. As time for bed arrived, it was problematic getting her night clothes on. Afterwards the fussing began. She would not go to bed. Then she told me to leave the room. So I retreated to the guest room as usual. I slept on and off, got up early, and went to our bed. I managed to get her back to bed. She awoke to use the restroom. I helped her and encouraged her to come back to bed. She stayed up. I got up later and we proceeded to take a shower. I shampooed her hair during the shower and helped her get dressed. Later I took in the Christmas lighting and decorations from outside and made dinner. She does have a good appetite. It's 8:45 pm now, and

I got her to go to bed. I will be turning in soon. She decided she wanted to go to Charleston on Friday, so we'll prepare for a few nights stay at Joe and Joy's. Lord, I pray for a restful night this evening.

January 4, 2012

We left early Friday morning to go to Charleston. The Lord gave us safe travel, arriving early afternoon and had a good time as we traveled. Soon after arriving at Joy's house, Joe and I went to the Ashley Towers to meet Brandon Thomas. We met Brandon, his mother, two brothers, his daughter and fiancée. We had a blessed time sharing with them and set the stage for baptism. The Lord granted us this privilege to honor his request to be baptized. I am grateful for this opportunity to minister to this young man. After the time of fellowship, we prayed and returned to Joe's house. Joy was preparing dinner; I went to shower and changed for a social that evening. When I left, Vera was having a good time at the dinner table. I left for a class social and met up with my classmates from 67'. It was a very good time. It was not the crowd they'd expected, but for those who arrived, we were elated seeing one another one more time. I returned home later and found Vera resting. That evening went well. On Saturday morning after breakfast, she and I went to see my mother and stayed for a while. Then we stopped by Piggly Wiggly to purchase some fruit and ginger ale for my uncle and then left to visit with my uncle Nathaniel in the nursing home. Vera stayed in the car, and I visited briefly with him. We left to find Herman

Whitney's Philly Cheesesteak restaurant, but it was closed. We returned to Joy's house for the remainder of the evening and got ready later for watch night services. Services went well, and Vera did alright during the services. We returned back to Joy's for a plate of "hopping John" and then to bed. The Lord gave us a new day and another Sunday morning to celebrate. We are glad to be into the New Year 2012. Vera and I went back to St. Matthews Baptist and met Dr. Brantley and gave him a copy of the book. Then we picked up Joyce and returned to Memorial for morning worship. Vera was very hesitant to go inside. Finally, we got inside the church and were seated in the back. She at times gets a bit agitated, but thank God we made it through the service. After church services, we stopped by the store and dropped Joyce home. We got back to Joy's house where we stayed for the remainder of the day. We had a restful evening, got to see more family who stopped by. It was just good being home in Charleston again. The next morning Joy prepared a sausage-egg biscuit for us and juice, and we left for Alabama. We stopped by Ronald and Carolyn Aaron's home and ate lunch. We fellowshipped for a while and then proceeded to head home. The Lord granted us safe travel, and we returned home finding David and everything else in good shape. It's good to be home. The last two days has been alright. Vera is a bit moody, but I love her just the same. I know this disease is robbing Vera of her personality, and it has been really depressing seeing her decline. Lord, grant us your grace and strength to get through this day. As the day warms up, I planned for us to walk around the neighborhood and then to check the mail at the post office. I tried to comfort Vera and she scratched me. I've tried to get her to watch the "price is right" show on television. Anyway, I pray the rest of the day goes well. I know we are going to have a great day. Lord, thank you for your strength. God, I give you the glory.

January 20, 2012

It has been 11 days since I made an entry. Thanking God for another day. I had a follow-up appointment with Dr. Franklin and was also treated for a cold and nasal drip. Other tests are alright. The doctor kept me on iron tablets to increase my hemoglobin and Zocor for cholesterol. Vera and I went to Hard Labor Creek State Park on Friday and remained for our board meeting on Saturday. She did well, commenting at times during the meeting, yet our friends understood her situation and were very cordial and loving towards her as always. We came back home Saturday evening. We turned in early in preparation for Sunday services. We got to Sunday school on time, and she sat next to me the whole time. After Sunday school, I escorted her to the sanctuary and she did well the entire service. I sat with her during the church meeting. Afterwards, I escorted her to the restroom, and then we left for home. We had a great dinner and relaxed for the rest of the day. We did a few things around the house on Monday, it being a holiday. I know one day this week I stayed in the guest room because she became upset. I often retreat to the guest room and found it to be a quiet time of refuge for me. The rest of this week went fine. I still will be there for Vera in whatever way I can to meet her needs. She went with me to the grocery store and ran a few errands around town. I appreciate her company and thank God each day for the time He has given us to share. We celebrated 43 years of marriage on Thursday January 19th and received calls from the kids and friends. Today is Friday. I was blessed to be the commencement speaker for Fortis College tonight. I am praying that the topic of "PASSION" will be an encouragement to the hearers. Vera will remain home with David. I am grateful for him being here with us.

January 27, 2012

Today is Friday, and the week was very interesting. I spent 2 nights in the guest room this week due to Vera making chewing noises with her teeth. Anyway, I am thankful for the day. God is good to us. We did not have Bible study Thursday due to the weather, so we stayed home and enjoyed the evening. I came into the room and awakened Vera, helped her get showered, and made breakfast for us. We got dressed and did some communications most of the morning. Late morning and early noon I raked the front yard. Boy, that was very tiring. Yet, it was a good exercise. Half of the way during my raking, I noticed Vera had left the front area. I went to the back yard and she was not there. I came back out front not seeing her and began to worry! I got a glimpse of her walking around the corner, down the loop. I called but she did not hear me. As I came down the loop I did not see her, wondering where she got to. She had walked quickly around to the North Loop, and it took me a bit to catch up with her. Needless to say, she was in a world of her own walking down the street and enjoying every moment. I was very concerned about her taking off without my knowing. We continued to walk into the other sub-division and came back home. We came into the house, and I prepared lunch for us. Then I returned to finish raking. Later that afternoon she took a ride with me to the bank. We came back home. We spent the rest of the day in the house. We had a very good dinner and I watched TV for a while. Vera was in the room rummaging as usual. She's in bed now, and I am soon to join her. Lord, I thank you for a great day. I'm counting it all joy!

January 31, 2012

Today is Tuesday afternoon, and all is well. The weekend was eventful, and we did well sharing together. I thank God for His grace. I have discovered that whatever assignment God has given is never greater than the grace He provides. Vera has lost a lot of ability to perform simple tasks. I cry inside as I observe her and try to help her in doing certain things. Sunday services went well, and she attended Sunday school and morning worship. David took us out to dinner after church, and we spent the rest of the day enjoying being home together. We did the Monday routine. This included walking around the neighborhood, something she likes doing. The day went well. As she went to bed, I found it troubling getting to sleep. I did some reading of the Scriptures, watched television a bit, and then turned in. She was grinding her teeth quite loudly so I retreated to the den and endured a rather restless night. She got up, and I heard her about the house. By that time David had come in from work. I noticed the bed was wet so I proceeded to turn on the showers. She took a shower, and I assisted her with the morning routine. God is still good and I thank Him for another day. The joy of the Lord is my strength.

February 4, 2012

Today has been a great day. We got things lined up at church in anticipation for the SPOLIWA's Annual Sunday School Conference. Friday went well, and Vera did swell all day. She was a bit tired at day's end, but overall she handled the conference both days in a splendid manner. I complimented her for her patience and contributions. I am grateful how many of our friends rallied around to assist her. That's family! We closed another successful Sunday school conference today. Vera did so well. We are home now and getting ready for bed. She seems to be doing fine. I am going to let her stay up as long as she wants to so when it is time to sleep she'll sleep the whole night through. Lord, it has been a blessed day, and You have met our needs in so many ways. Thank You my God, and I count it all joy.

February 20, 2012

WOW! It's been a week since my last entry. It has been quite busy. Vera has done quite well this past week. We've had some good times. We've been celebrating her birthday all month. Her birthday day is February 5th. As a matter-of-fact we went to SHONEY'S for breakfast this morning and had a great time. She allowed me to put a quick relaxer in her hair last week. It helped! She did hit the sitter on Saturday afternoon unsuspectingly! I do hope that never occurs again. It's a challenge at times when someone not familiar comes over. There are times she treats the kids a bit as strangers as well. Lord, I asked You to give us both what we need for each day. Thank You for Your grace and mercy. I am going to let her help me with vacuuming and dusting this morning.

February 29, 2012

Today finds me dealing with some very strong emotions. The last 24 hours have been really a challenge. I see Vera declining more and more. She said that I was not her husband, and she wished I would get out of here. Earlier this week she told me not to sleep in the bedroom, yet she never went to sleep. I got up early in morning and finally carted her off to bed. Yesterday was extremely difficult! She seems withdrawn and stood in the kitchen for hours, not wanting to get her night clothing on. I changed into my night clothing and finally brought her into the room and, while fussing, she let me help her change her clothing. She fussed at me to no end; I felt so hurt, starting to cry within, crying out to God for help. Again, she kicked me out the room, and I was so frustrated I left for the den. The Lord awakened me about 2:30 am, and I went to check on her. She had water running in the sink, overflowing to the bathroom floor. Thank God it did not make it to the carpeting. I dried the floors, changed her clothing, and finally got her to go to bed. I cleared the bathroom and put the wet towels in the washing machine. She went to sleep. I came into the bed with her and went to sleep. She got up around 5 AM and walked around. I got up to run the showers for her, and she was still complaining. I put more clothes in the washing machine and dried the others. I saw where the bed was wet, so I changed all the linen. I left the bed open to air out and waited until the fitted sheets were dried; I had a clean one and in the quest to dry the floor, I used it. Anyway, I prepared breakfast. Vera is sitting at the table now. I finally got her to eat her breakfast. She's sleepy so I took her back to the bedroom to take a nap in the chair. I went to the bathroom to get the Ridex and found underneath the counter was wet. I took everything out and dried the counter's shelving. I threw out some things we hadn't used and replaced the rest. Vera got up, and I tried to get her to go back and rest in the chair. Seeing it may escalate I left for the kitchen and back to journaling again. It's hard, and I ask the Lord for help and strength for this day.

Patrick is due in tonight. Mel arrives late tomorrow night. I hope Vera allows them to help her while I am away. I feel I need this break because I am getting impatient, and I try not to let her disease cause me to react to her in an unloving way. Lord, grant me your grace for this day. I have a few more things to do around the house to get it in good shape.

Lord, I give this day back to you and pray to find time to rest throughout this day.

March 1, 2012

Wednesday went really great. Vera and I packed a lunch and spent some quality time at the Village Green Park. After eating lunch, we walked the trail for about 30 minutes. It turned out to be a very great day. It felt so relaxing compared to the day before. I thank the Lord for this change and truly appreciate how Vera's handling the day. She went with me to pick Patrick up from the airport and took to having him home in a very joyful manner. We ate spaghetti and salad for dinner and had a good time talking. As the evening went along I saw Vera getting sleepy. She allowed me to assist her getting her night clothing on. She rested in the chair in our bedroom while Pat and I talked for a bit. I went back to check on her, and she went to bed. I came to bed later, and the Lord blessed us with a good night sleep. Praise God for a blessed day. The Lord awakened me this morning, and I spent some quiet time with Him. Vera got up and came into the living room. I greeted her and helped her in showering and getting dressed. I took a shower next. Afterwards, I prepared breakfast for us and we enjoyed the time at the table. I read a devotional to her, and we prayed together. She does not pray like she once did, mostly quiet and listens. I perceive a change in her area of dialogue, but I thank God the more for the time He is allowing us to share together. Pat got up later. David had arrived while I was tending to Mom. The morning went well. I spent time going over our budget and went to the bank. Upon returning home we three talked some more. She seems to be more engaged in conversation and for that I am glad. She went with me to Office Depot and the Dollar Tree. We returned home, and I got myself together for the trip to Texas. I took another shower and trimmed my beard and hair. Pat went to Starbucks and retuned later. I put my baggage in the car and around 2 PM Vera and Pat took me to the airport. On the way to the airport she was very engaged in conversation. I kissed her after arriving at the airport. Patrick prayed for us, and I went to catch my flight. I called home after arriving in Atlanta. Mom seems to be doing fine as Pat was preparing dinner. I pray the rest of the evening goes well, that Vera will have a restful night, and allowed the kids to help her. Having missed my connection, I went to TGI Friday's for dinner and met Elliot, from Pittsburg, PA who was en-route to Huntsville, AL. I felt the Lord arranged that dinner time so he and I could talk. I was led to share some insight for living with this young man and will be praying for he and Tara, his girlfriend, whom he plans to marry. I am awaiting now to board my connecting flight. I feel my trip was fruitful already. I arrived to San Antonio late that night and was blessed to arrive safely. I had a good night's sleep.

March 2, 2012

The Lord awoke me this morning, and I had some quiet time with Him. I called home to check on Vera. She had not allowed the kids to help her change. She did not eat very much today. Finally, this evening she let Mel and Nita help her wash and change her clothing. I pray Saturday will be better. The Lord blessed me today by awarding me the Order of the Golden Microscope Award (OGM). It is the highest award given to a Medical Technologist by AMT. I was speechless, thanking the ALSSAMT for nominating me for such an honor. I look forward to the ceremonies this summer, Lord willing. We had a fruitful day of board meeting. I took a visit to Fort Sam Houston METC and had a very enjoyable social time this evening with my AMT colleagues. We have a full day tomorrow. I am thankful to belong to such a great organization as AMT and to have been able for the past eight years to work at the board level. I am back in my room now. I spoke with David, Nita and Pat this evening and all is well. I pray for a good night sleep.

March 5, 2012

I arrived home safely on Sunday morning. Pat and Mel had arrived home safely. Renita was here upon my return, and she left shortly afterwards. I am blessed to have my children pitch in when I need them. I love them so very much. Thanks be to God for His grace and mercy. It's Monday morning, and Vera and I are sitting at the breakfast table. Vera was a bit agitated this morning, but I think it will pass, and I pray we'll have a great day. I missed her while in Texas. Lord, I pray you will go before us and direct our paths. Please keep our pathway straight. I trust to get caught up on some home things and will review my to do list for this week.

March 29, 2012

My entries appear to be getting fewer. It's been over a week since I listed anything in the diary. There are fewer entries, but things are still moving right along. I see my wife's cognitive abilities weaning away. I may ask her to do something, and she appears to be somewhat confused. So I have to give her a nudge. She seems to want to be at home more often. Should we go some places, she is hesitant to go inside and her steps get slower and stiffer. I keep trying! We went to Nita's house yesterday to deliver a cake for Sam. We had not been there long when she was ready to go back home. She said she had a lot of work to do. I didn't argue and tried to accommodate her and keep her happy. There are times I still am accused or blamed or called a liar, yet I thank God for the day and the trials. Lord, I pray in Jesus' mighty name for total healing for Vera, her being delivered from dementia. It's slow and compromising her cognitive abilities. I still help her daily with bathing, restroom use, clothing and meal preparation. I don't mind; we both are in this together: in sickness and in health! I pray for grace and strength for each day. It has been a good week, and I trust to continue moving forward.

April 8, 2012

The trip to Columbus, Georgia was eventful as I was delayed twice due to highway construction, yet I met with the Miller Motte Clinical Laboratory students and staff and they were pleased having the proclamation signing experience with the mayor. I returned home. Vera was cared for by

Jennifer Swift, a Christian young lady. She seems to take to this home health young lady quite well. I hope to retain her services at other times too. Wednesday morning I went to participate in a signing ceremony with the Clinical Laboratory students from Baptist South Lab School and the mayor of Montgomery. That was a very encouraging visit. Thursday morning Vera and I went to sister Jeanette's McKinzie's school where her class of students presented an Easter presentation. It was very informative, and the gospel message was clearly presented. Humility services at Sanctuary went well. Vera was quite restful and seems to enjoy the service. Friday evening we went to dine with Nita, Sam, Mel, Em, Mari and Lil Em. Things went well until it was time for us to be seated. Vera was very agitated and did not want to move. It took everything I had to encourage her to get up. Then she wanted to go home. I was about to take her home. Nita, Mel, and Sam came over, and I persuaded her to come with us to the table. She did and walked very "stiff-like" as I helped her towards where the family was sitting. She enjoyed the time, ate a good meal, and we left encouraged having stayed. She and I drove back to Millbrook. Saturday morning we ate breakfast with the Aundrey and Nadine at Shoney's. The time was well spent, and she was very conversational. The night went well. She allowed me to help her put on her night clothes. I noticed she got up a bit early as it seems to be her regular routine. When I got up I read some and then took a shower. I prepared breakfast, and we ate together. Afterwards, she allowed me to get her dressed. We headed to church not knowing what will come of it. Upon arriving, she did not want to get out of the car. I tried unsuccessfully; she was not coming out. After a few members stopped by to encourage her to come inside, she told them a few choice words. I said, Lord have mercy. I wrote a check and gave it to Pastor McKenzie to deposit during offering time. I took Vera home. She hesitated to get out of the car after we arrived home. She was still a bit upset with me, but I pressed on and changed her clothes. She came in the kitchen where I was. I was being quiet, not wanting to cause any more problems. She smiled at me. What could I do after seeing her smile at me? I felt warm within. I accepted her smiling and thanked God for it. I took out what I might prepare for dinner, took care of some finance matters, and made some apple cinnamon tea for us. She is resting now in the living room. I started washing clothes, prepared the grocery list, and worked a Sudoku puzzle. Lord, help me not to get upset; this disease is very devastating, and I need your grace and peace to support Vera during this season. I pray the rest of the day goes well.

Dear friends and readers, this has been nearly two years of journaling to give you an idea of how our days have been. Through it all God has been gracious unto us. He has taught me to number my days and make good use of the time He has given Vera and me together. I will take the liberty to write how things have been more recently.

May 9, 2012

The last few days have been quite relaxing, and I thank God that Vera appears to be doing alright at this time. We have not fussed in a while, and she allows me to tend to her without controversy. She visited the optometrist on yesterday, and this morning we went to Affordable Eyewear to order 2 pairs of glasses. I have worked in the yard recently, and she spends time sitting and watching me work, my supervisor. I got the radio and tune into a favorite station, WVAS-FM 90.7; she enjoys the music. Lord, I thank you. I am praying we will have a restful night this evening.

June 6, 2012

For some reason, yesterday afternoon was a challenge. After we walked in the evening, upon returning to the house, Vera was hesitant to come inside. I do not know why or what brought this behavior on, yet I tried to be patient. I had to push her into the house to her not wanting me to touch her. That went on into the night. I did manage to get her pajamas on, and she went to bed. Today, it was alright. She needed to be changed this morning. I gave her a sponge bath and dressed her. I prepared some breakfast and the day was on. She has been a bit more hesitant in doing anything around the house. Today went fairly smooth. She accompanied me on a few errands. We ate dinner together which she enjoyed. We went walking for about 30 minutes. I prepared a piece of carrot cake for her. She allowed me to assist her in putting on her pajamas. She's in the den now, and I hope she will go to bed soon. Lord, I thank you for a good day. We have been talking throughout the day about attending Bible camp next week. I pray she'll be excited about next week. It will afford her and me the opportunity to spend some quality time together. I plan to attend the support group meeting at Fraser tomorrow morning. It has been very encouraging, and I gain strength from this environment. Sue Cobb leads the discussion and does an excellent job facilitating. God is so good, and I count this season and experience a joy!

June 9, 2012

These past few days have been well. The meeting at Fraser was super. It's good to be able to share in a forum like this one; it is very supportive. Vera has been doing fine. She still tends to stand in a single spot and not want to sit when I ask. I take it a step at a time. She went with me to run a few errands Friday morning. She did well at Bible study and remained for choir rehearsal. I thank God for how things are coming along. Lord, I pray that you will continue to grant Vera the ability to enjoy our outings. We leave for Bible camp in the morning, and I trust she'll do well for the next five nights. Each day is somewhat different, but I pray for God's grace to respond to every situation with love and kindness. We will be heading to bed soon, and I pray for a restful night.

June 20, 2012

These past two days have been rather good. Vera tends to be more stand-offish. She hesitates when I call or may not respond at all when I call her. I am adjusting to this situation and praying for more understanding to not rush her. She is slowing down in her response to my requests. I am concerned, Lord, because I am seeing more decline. Other times I am taken back by her smile and jovial demeanor. I am still taking one day at a time. We had some good weekend trips. We go to visit Carmela and family next week for 2 days and then on to Charleston. I hope Vera does alright for that trip. Then she, David and I leave for San Antonio on July 7th. I pray she does well for this lengthy trip. Oh, well, I will make an effort now to get her night clothes on.

July 4, 2012

It has been a week since my last entry into the diary. The time spent at Mel's was very restful and enjoyable. I am praying that Em's medical issues will be cleared in God's time. Vera did well with the visit. Mel took us to Lake Norman, and it was such a beautiful place. I hope there will be another time to visit this place. We left Friday afternoon for Charleston. The weekend with my classmates was most memorable. We had a great time. They supported us with a book signing, and I am thankful to God for the open door. It was great being with family and friends. We got to see Aunt Gladys and my mom. The time was restful and a blessing.

Then we made the trip to Shreveport and the next day drove down to San Antonio. I thank God for safe travel. It has been a very enjoyable week. Vera has done quite well to being here. It's a challenge for her not being at home, but she has done well, and I am thankful. It feels so good being amongst our friends from AMT. I was honored at a special dinner tonight. I thank Josephine Harden for helping with Vera, and she has consented to be with her tomorrow while I am attending a committee meeting. She and Hattie Gallon are jewels, and I appreciate their friendship. Vera's in bed now, and I am soon to follow. It's been a good day. The award convocation is tomorrow, and I pray for wisdom in making my comments on tomorrow night. Lord, I thank You for a good day.

July 16, 2012

It's been a while and a very busy AMT Convention. We had a great time. The Lord gave us safe travel over 1800 miles round-trip. Vera did quite well and now we are back home. It felt good being back at Sanctuary on Sunday. We spent most of yesterday and today in the house. I got all the washing of clothes done, and I have a few more house chores to do. I came down with a cold on our way home Saturday. I saw a clinician today who prescribed some meds that seem to be working well. I've been out of the kitchen for a while. I enjoyed the break. I think I will prepare a meatloaf for dinner tonight.

August 6, 2012

It's been a busy 2 weeks and yet enjoyable. I thank the Lord for getting me through the sinus infection. I am feeling much better. It was good to be home resting. Vera has done very well during times at church, Bible study, and morning worship services. We attended 3 nights of VBS and concluded on Thursday Bible study which was well attended. We stayed for choir rehearsal waiting for Jeanette. Vera has done great these past 2 weeks. Nita and I attended the annual Alzheimer's conference and gained some valuable information. The weekend was good. I hear Vera groaning more. When I ask her how she's feeling she'll say alright. Her steps are getting slower. When calling her, it takes her a while to respond. I have to push her and help move her along. She tends to rest and nap more and more. I enjoy spending time with her, but I realize I need to TCOY: (Take Care Of Yourself). This is a phrase that we are encouraged to employ as caregivers. So, I will be sure to get sufficient rest. I love Vera and am committed to ensure she has everything she needs. Lord, I pray for wisdom to make wise choices regarding Vera's care. She rode with me this morning to get the remaining props and delivered them to Camilla Baptist Church School. We returned home and had lunch and is resting now.

August 11, 2012

Tuesday morning Laura Hedgecock, a home health nurse from Home Helpers, came over to stay with Vera as I traveled to Fort Rucker. I appreciate Laura in that she is a Christian who loves the Lord, and Vera took well to her being in our home. She often prays over Vera and reads Scripture to her. This is a blessing. I received a call from Carmela that Emmett has gotten critical, and she wanted us to come to Charlotte. I returned back to Millbrook after having settled my appointment at Fort Rucker. I called her back to get updates on Emmett. Vera and I left Wednesday morning en-route to Charlotte to be with Mel, the kids and Em's mother, Dorothy Harris.

Vera has done well these past 5 days, and I thank God for sustaining her. We are all turning in now. I am praying we'll get a telephone call with good news. I am praying that Emmett's condition remains stable. Lord, thank you for this season, and I pray You will show yourself strong on our behalf and meet Emmett's need this weekend. Vera and I returned home yesterday. She did well on our traveling, and it's a joy being back. Yet, our hearts and minds are still reflecting and praying for Emmett. We pray for a good night's rest. I pray for Carmela, Dorothy, Shomari and Lil Em that you will grant them peace tonight and victory tomorrow.

September 8, 2012

The news came on the evening of August 29th that my son-in-law, Emmett, passed away. This was very shocking to us in that we expected him to recover. The Lord took him home to be with Him. Vera, David, and I came to Charlotte the very next day. It was so touching seeing Mel, Dorothy and the kids tearful and grief-stricken, yet God would bring comfort to our hearts. I am praying for Mel, Shomari and Lil Em to get through this season. Vera seems to have handled this crisis alright.

Vera and I left for Millbrook on Wednesday September 12, 2012.

October 3, 2012

Praise the Lord! We had a safe trip back home. I got to help Mel out with a few things around the house. I enjoyed so much being there with her, Mari and Lil Em. Vera did very well being out-of-pocket for 5 days. Mel is coming along and getter better daily. We thank God. Vera's back in familiar territory this evening, and I pray we have a good evening tonight. I just asked her if she's glad to be home, and she said, "Yes!" Our trip back was good. We had a good time traveling, singing, and chatting. It was just good to be together, and I thank God for everything. We plan to return on next week Friday to Mel's house. Renita will be going back to spend the weekend with Mel. I am grateful for this season and having the time and resources to make the trips to visit with Mel and the kids. Thank you Lord! Through all of this Vera's responding relatively well.

October 24, 2012

It's been awhile since my last entry, and I thank God for His grace. Things have been coming along reasonably well. Vera still has a tendency to hesitate at times. I notice more avoidance and slowing down when we approach other people. She even tends to turnaround or stop walking. She engages billboard signs as we travel. I perceive she is reacting to the portraits of people. I have to reassure her at times and speak to her quietly to not engage people. Our trip to the commissary was great as she talked to a lot of people in a casual manner. She was retested for her mammogram, and it resulted in a negative test. I thank God, for indeed I was a bit anxious. I am the more thankful that she does not have any other medical issues. Overall, we're taking one day at a time, and I am grateful to God for His goodness. I leave for Chicago tomorrow, Thursday, for 2 days. I pray things go well as Pat and Nita will come over to be with their Mom. I have asked Home Helpers to send someone for Friday morning. Vera is resting on the den sofa now. I pray the rest of the evening goes well and that she will not react negatively to Pat being here when he arrives.

October 26, 2012

I left Mom with Pat on yesterday, and she did well. Of course she was hesitant to let Pat change her. I was glad I requested Home Helpers to send Laura. She arrived, and Vera allowed her to wash her, changed clothes, use the restroom and got her refreshed for the day. Lord, I thank You for your provision of help. Pat leaves in the morning, Saturday, to drive back to Columbus. I pray for his safe travel. Nita has arrived at the house and will be there until I return on Saturday night. I am thankful for my children's willingness to help out and give their support. I am rested in mind and heart now. God is good, and I count it all joy. I praise God for my children.

December 3, 2012

It has been a good day today. Vera had an increased problem with incontinence today. I had to assist her several times by ensuring she is cleaned and undergarments changed. She hit me once during the time I was helping her and tended to be more argumentative. Yet, I asked the Lord for more grace and patience to help her. I love Vera!

Her neurologist approved a request for a handicap window decal, and I went to get it and found that there was no cost. They gave us 2 hanging decals. The rest of the day we spent around the house. I did some more work in cleaning the den. We had the Volvo taken to be repaired. We returned home and just finished eating. I plan to relax the rest of the evening. Vera's tapping the floor more often, and her shaking has increased as well. I am concerned and shed tears during those times. God already knows!

December 6, 2012

This morning Vera and I are sitting at the breakfast table. I am tearing up as I look at her and remembered how she was. Lord, you have given us many wonderful years together. Now, Lord, in this season of affliction I asked for Your grace to help in this time of need. I thank you for this day and that things are as well as they are. I helped her brush her teeth and wash her face this morning. We ate breakfast together. Again, she appears at times to not recognize me, but I press on in the strength God provides to ensure that her every need is met. I plan to attend a support group Christmas fellowship later this morning. It will be a welcomed respite for a couple of hours. I love my wife and pray she too will experience a good day. Bible study will convene this evening at 6 PM. I am praying for a fruitful time as we get close to completing the Red Sea

Rules study book. Vera has done well at Bible classes. She is still hesitant when it comes to coming into Sanctuary. I am praying God will give her what she needs for this day.

I am sitting at the laptop preparing an article for the newsletter. Vera is sitting in an adjacent chair, patting her feet, pulling her earring, and groaning. She looks at me with hazy eyes. She says she's tired. She sings as the television is playing Christmas songs. I do not know what to do. I have tears in my eyes. I do not know how to help her. I ask her to stand and hold my hands. I ask her to embrace me. I feel so helpless as I see my mate of 44 years slowly slipping away. My heart is breaking, and I feel sad. I try to share with her that maybe we can get the kids and grandkids something for Christmas. She does not fully understand. This will be a different Christmas as Vera does not comprehend its meaning much anymore. Lord, this disease has taken my mate, and time is slipping away. I must cherish every moment we have together. Sometimes I'm up, and sometimes I'm down, but I will enjoy every moment. She went in the den and sat on the sofa and continues to shake. Lord, would you give her relief from this affliction! Lord, it is hard to count it joyful when I see how she is, yet I will still trust you!

January 1, 2013

Praise the Lord for this New Year! The last two days have been good. Vera has done well. She has an increased tendency now to stand still and sing. I often try to get her to engage in conversation. She hesitates at times to come into the house. I see an increase in this area as well. Nonetheless, I thank God for His grace and mercy. If the Lord allows, we will celebrate 44 years of marriage on January 19, 2013. I love her very much. I fixed one of her favorite breakfasts this morning: pancakes, turkey bacon, eggs, and hazelnut coffee with Irish creamer. She seems content to just stand. She talks with herself more often, but I am determined for us to enjoy every moment God has given to us. I love Vera! Incontinency has increased, and I pray for godly and daily wisdom to assist her as best I can. The day went well overall. We spent the day inside. I pray for a good night's rest. Vera's in bed now. I am finishing up a few things and will be turning in shortly. Lord, I thank you for a great day.

February 10, 2013

It has been a frantic week. I had a scare early Tuesday morning (February 5th) and felt so helpless as my head felt so dizzy and out of control, My equilibrium was off, and I had David call EMT. Renita and Sam took me to the emergency room, and the diagnosis may be vertigo/inner ear issues. The clinician recommended I see an ENT clinician. I was given an appointment for February 26th which I feel is too far off. So I will call in the morning to see about a closer appointment. I still feel quite off at times. Even now as I type I feel dizziness coming on. Thank God Vera has been good through all of this. I should have results from a prostate biopsy tomorrow. So much is going on, and I am a bit anxious about that too; but Lord, I give it all to you. You already know! I am grateful for your many blessings and say thank you for watching over me and my family. I pray we'll have a restful night this evening.

We were able to attend the SPOLIWA Sunday school conference. Pastor McKenzie did the driving. I was still able to give the opening message. This was the first time I ever preached sitting down. Things went well, and I thank God for being a part of this ministry. Everyone had safe travel thanks to God our Savior.

March 3, 2013

I am sitting in the Hartsfield-Jackson Airport awaiting my flight to Montgomery that has been delayed. In everything give thanks! I am just returning from San Diego. Nita and Mel came to stay with Mom while I was away. This was my last spring board meeting with AMT. I come off the board this summer during the meeting in Pittsburgh. Vera did well with the girls being home. I miss her and look forward to seeing her this evening. I think I will take her fishing this week if the weather is warm enough. It will be good to be home again. Lord, I thank you for the AMT journey as one of its leaders and having had the pleasure of serving the 60,000 plus members. I am grateful and thankful for You, Oh God, and Your divine provision of everything that we need. I pray to embark on a pathway of victory, prayer and passion. I am praying to take back what the enemy may have caused me to miss. I am praying and fasting for Vera's health and asking God to keep her and deliver and restore her from dementia. I am looking forward to attending the support group meeting this

Thursday. I missed the last two. I have enjoyed the camaraderie. Lord, use this season of affliction for your glory. Thank you Lord!

March 20, 2013

It has been a trying day. Vera is having more soft stools, and I have had to clean her more often these past two days. I was concerned earlier that she was not having a bowel movement regularly, but now she is having a problem with this. I have to change her more often and wipe and wash her to make sure she remains clean and smelling good. Lord, I ask for your grace and tenderness as I care for Vera. I cannot get mad or upset, even though there are times I may. I understand that she cannot help her condition. I perceive more decline. She tends to talk to herself more often than before. I must take things a moment at a time. She makes sounds more often now, and I think she may be in pain. This affliction of dementia is so devastating, and I ask God to be gracious unto my wife. Help me, Lord, to help Vera and make sure her every moment is spent well.

I have several outings next month. April will be a busy month. Nita said she will come home to cover for me while I attend a board meeting in Mobile for a couple of hours. I am thankful for her support and her being nearby. I was invited by my Caribbean colleagues to speak at their allied health meeting in Nassau, Bahamas. However, I think I may not go. The children have been very supportive of my fall and spring board meetings. I would like the time to make this trip, but I think I may decline and not burden them to have to take more time off. I appreciate all their efforts. Vera is in bed now; I have changed her twice tonight. I hope she does alright until morning. I hope she will do alright and that her stomach will be settled. Lord, thank you for this day. I pray to take one day at a time. Your will be done! The joy of the Lord is my strength.

April 4, 2013

The last few days have really been good. Joe and Joy came to visit with us, and I thank God for allowing them to spend time with us. It felt good laughing and sharing together. Vera enjoyed the time as well, and we did a lot of laughing. She ate well. We went to the Chinese restaurant, Ding How, and Vera ate 2 plates full of food. I thank God she has been doing alright lately. She and I have been smiling and laughing a lot. I appreciate her and am cherishing these times and days together. I attended my support group today and met a lady whose husband had passed away from early onset of dementia, the same affliction that Vera now has. We talked and encouraged each other. The group has been quite helpful to attend as we share heart to heart how we are doing, and no one feels out-of-place. Later Vera and I attended bible study. We had a good time and have returned home now. I had a good time talking with grandkids, Shomari and Lil Em, over the phone tonight as well. Vera and I plan to visit with them in 2 weeks. We both have on our PJ's. I pray God grants us a good night sleep.

April 10, 2013

I thank you Lord for another day. I woke up yesterday feeling a bit light-headed. My equilibrium seemed off. I took it slow for most of the day. I didn't do anything strenuous. Last night I slept in the chair in the bed room. I trust it'll subside. I have a clinician's appointment on Friday morning, and I will inform her of this latest episode.

April 28, 2013

The time spent with Mel and the kids was very good. Vera did well being away for 5 days. We had safe travel back home, thank God. I am a bit overwhelmed this evening. Over the last six months I have been having some health issues: prostate problems, yet the biopsy was negative, thank God; dizzy spells and equilibrium issues, yet no specific diagnosis; and I've been put on low dose of blood pressure meds. Now I have developed a swelling on the right side of my jaw and neck area. I need to get a clinician to assess what's going on. On top of that Vera has been my primary focus, and Lord, I do not need to get sick because I am her primary caregiver. Please help me to overcome these issues so I might be in good health and strength to take care of my wife. Every day brings a new challenge, yet Lord, I trust you to take care of us. I will do all I need to do, but I must rely upon You. I realize that we are getting older. Lord, I am thankful for each and every day you have given Vera and me to share together. Many of our classmates have gone off the scene. I have had several family members who also have gone on too. As we get to move on in age I think often about leaving this side. The timeline of life is drawing ever so close. I praise God for the hope that I have in the Lord Jesus Christ, yet Lord, I want to remain in the center of your will. Please give me grace and strength sufficient for each day.

This morning I decided to call again for a closer appointment and was directed to go to an urgent care facility. I was able to be seen this morning, and I thank God for this care center. The clinician examined me, ordered blood tests, administered a steroid shot and gave me a prescription for Augmentin to take the next 10 days. I already feel the difference in that some of the swelling has subsided. He also recommended that I rest for two full days of which I have curbed back certain activities. Thank God for His goodness and mercy! I rested. I did go to an eye appointment, and the optometrist said she may confer with my primary care doctor regarding a referral for further neurology work-up. In addition, I still have some swelling on the right side. I pray the antibiotic will enable it to subside. I am not doing anything strenuous. Lord, You already know so I leave this to you and will await your deliverance.

May 15, 2013

Mother's Day went well; Vera did well at church services. Afterwards she, David and I met Nita and Sam at Ding How for dinner. We had a restful day. Monday, Vera and went walking. That afternoon Elaine came and spent time with Vera while I went to an appointment. When I returned home,

I chatted with Elaine and later prepared dinner. Vera stayed in the den asleep and did not want to be moved so I went to bed. I woke up a little later, and she was up in the den. She did come back to the bedroom. I helped change her into her pajamas, and we went to sleep. She got up again around 4:30 AM; I stayed in bed and then got up. I prepared some tea then gave Vera a "birdie bath." David was off today, so he kept Vera while I went to a follow-up urology appointment. I also went to the hospital laboratory because I needed to get blood work in preparation for a CT scan tomorrow morning. Nadine said she would come and stay with Vera while I make this appointment. Seems like these past 6 months have been a challenge for me medically, but I thank God for each day; He is in control!

May 19, 2013

CT scan revealed something suspect so I was scheduled to see an ENT clinician. At my Friday afternoon appointment with ENT, the clinician took several samples from the enlarged area for pathology. He also scoped my right nostril. My follow-up appointment is Thursday afternoon. Lord, I pray for a favorable report. I am feeling alright, just a little anxious regarding my follow-up appointment. Lord, I commit everything to you. I am praying for a restful evening tonight.

May 23, 2013

On my return appointment, I received some bad news today. My neck has a squamous cell carcinoma. Lord, I don't know what to do with this news. I was advised I would need surgery and radiation. I commit this news and situation to You. I trust you with everything that pertains to me. I leave it in your hands. I am concerned the more for Vera and her care. I pray you will take care of her should this be my time to leave this side. Your will be done. I ask for more time. I remember Hezekiah asked You, and he was given 15 more years. Lord, I pray that your perfect will for my life be manifested. Lord, please have your way and grant me what I need to endure this affliction. Please take away the anxiety that I feel now and help me to trust you.

May 28, 2013

Lord, I went to the Kirkland Clinic today and the clinician took more samples. I pray we'll get a favorable report on Friday. I am scheduled for surgery on June 12th. I asked you, my God, to work on my behalf. I don't know what brought this on, but I need you to move in a mighty way and help me. Vera appeared to have had a good day. I commit all things back to you. Please give us a restful night.

June 11, 2013

I have to be at UAB at 5AM in the morning with a probable surgery time of 7AM. Lord, I give myself to you. I abide under the shadow of your Almighty wings. Please give your angels charge over me. I pray for success with this surgery and recovery being a great prognosis. This is new to me, Lord, and I ask for healing and that you will bring me through. I need to be in place for Vera, and I need your strength and healing virtue to minister to and through me during this time. Please enable me to return to this laptop with a testimony of your hand of grace. I pray Vera will allow Mel to assist her while I am hospitalized. Lord, I pray there will be no problems in this area and that Vera will be cooperative just as she allows me to tend to her as well.

June 14, 2013

Well, I thank God. He brought me through surgery successfully, and now I am home resting. I am so thankful for Mel, Nita and Sam who are here with Vera and me ensuring that things went well. I pray God's continual blessing upon them for their assistance. I have a follow-up appointment next Friday with the surgeon, and I suppose we'll discuss the course of treatment. Lord, I thank you for keeping me; I thank you for the prayers of so many. Vera is doing alright and allowing the girls to tend for her. Lord, I ask you for a successful recovery period. Today was good. The girls are ensuring that I rest and not do any work. They are answering all my calls so I can rest completely. I appreciate their sacrifice and service. Vera's in bed now, and I am soon to follow. Lord, I ask you to give us all a restful evening.

Well my dear friends, I found it difficult to conclude this chapter. However, I have gone full circle from the point of caring for Vera until I was being cared for myself. As I pen this and the other chapters to follow, it is the spring of 2014.

God has been good to us. I desired to share what the experience has been for my family and me. God has used so many friends during this season, and I had to learn how to receive when others wanted to serve us. It has been humbling, yet I thank God for the journey. I will continue to journal. I trust this has been an enlightening chapter for you.

Years before Vera was diagnosed with early onset dementia, she wrote a tribute to me for our 30th wedding anniversary. It is something very dear to my heart that I feel reflects her thoughts towards me over the years. I thought it fitting to end this chapter with this letter.

AN OPEN LETTER TO
Paul Charles Brown
My Husband, My Lover and My Best Friend!
By Vera L. Brown

My darling husband, it was thirty years ago that God, through His Divine Providence brought our two lives together and united us as husband and wife. That day was the day that God's plans for our lives were set in motion. We had no way of knowing that our walk together in life would be as sweet as it has been, nor could we know that we would reach this milestone of 30 beautiful years of companionship.

When we were in the sixth grade you, a fledgling young man, and I, a shy snickering little girl, did not know it at the time, but looking back, our God was working out a plan with us in mind. We became acquainted and became friends.

Somewhere along the line something happened. I recalled that in my sophomore year of high school, you asked me to marry you. Of course, I wanted to say yes, but I said, "My mother will not let me." So we had to wait a few more years.

Our love for each other began to blossom and grow. We had our ups and downs. There were disappointments and challenges that we had to face, but our love sustained us. God, our Father, did not see us for what we were, but for what we were to become for Him. He looked beyond our faults and saw that He could make something beautiful out of our lives once we yielded ourselves to Him.

On January 19, 1969, you and I stood side by side, with our hands joined together, before Reverend Grady in the Morris Brown AME Church parsonage in Charleston, South Carolina. I do believe that I heard Angels singing during the ceremony, and they have been singing ever since.

We accepted our Lord and Savior, Jesus Christ as the Lord and Master of our lives and home. He was first in your life, and I saw the joy you possessed and I wanted it too. It was because of your beautiful character, the fruit of the Spirit that I saw in you that made me want it too. You led me gently and patiently to Christ, and I thank you very much!

Paul, this Thirtieth wedding anniversary marks another milestone in our beautiful relationship. It is hard to believe that 30 years have passed. It seems that our journey has only just begun. You make me feel very special. You, with your charming ways and beautiful smile make me feel like a brand new bride every day. It is a lot like the Lord's mercies, they are new every morning!

You have always made me feel loved. And, you know, it is not the big things you do, but the small things, the daily things, the thoughtful things, the personal things. How, that even in a crowd, I still feel that I am the only one that is important. Even though I know that God is definitely first in your life, and your work at the Camp is your life's blood, you have never made me to feel in second place to any of your priorities, but have succeeded in letting me know without a shadow of a doubt, that I, your LOVIE, am an equal partner, a true companion, a pal and indeed the joy of your life. THANK YOU so much for that!

You, my love, are a true Pastor, and you are a gentleman. I love you as my pastor, and I love you as my husband. I am trying to express my thoughts to you, and it is taking so much time and words. You know that I am not one for words. But after thirty lovely years of walking together as partners, and raising five children, and the Lord blessing us with four grands, I have so much for which to be grateful, and so much to say.

After years of receiving your tokens of affections, love letters, many of which I still have today, and your many love notes that you leave in special places so that I could find them, I can't help but be a little verbose on this special occasion!

You are always the kind gentleman who opens doors and helps me in and out of the vehicle and house. You are the thoughtful one who remembers the special occasions with candies and flowers and cards! You take the time to give me a break from the kitchen by taking me out to dinner as often as you can (and you know that Red Lobster is my favorite spot). You are the considerate one, who never complains about things being out of place, but pitches in and helps with the housecleaning. You are the introspective one who seems to sense my innermost thoughts and gives the right words at the right time that lift my soul on high.

Now for you, my partner, my prince, my love, I want you to know that you are indeed the joy of my life. You are like a GIANT OAK TREE whose branches spread far and wide, providing shade and shelter and even food for all within your sphere of influence. Your roots tap the rich nourishment from the Word of God by which you grow daily. You, like the oak, whose roots seek water to sustain itself, are careful to draw daily drafts of WATER from the SPRING of LIVING WATERS. You, Paul, are my PRINCE.

Your character is liken to pure gold. Your words are words that one can count on to be dependable. Thirty years, huh! Hard to believe! You are not getting older, you are just getting better and I thank God for you my love, and I praise Him every day for His sustaining power and His manifested love for us!

So, my dear Paul, if your eyes are still dry, and you have composed yourself, I will conclude this open letter to you with these words of poetry:

*Thirty years of marital bliss, have been like heaven
here on earth,
Your soft touch and gentle kiss, the fun the
laughter and the mirth,
Have made me feel like a queen, willing to serve
and do my part
Guided by Hands, though unseen, yet willing to
give you my entire heart.
Thank you for choosing me to share your life, to be
your companion and your wife.*

Yours forever,

VERA

"Say it With Poetry," By Nat Greene
Copyright 1/14/99

Chapter 3

IN SICKNESS AND IN HEALTH

"Therefore shall a man leave his father and mother, and shall cleave unto his wife: and they shall become one flesh." (Genesis 2:24)

I grew up on Gadsden Green Projects, known as "Back the Green" in Charleston, South Carolina. It was on a sunny summer afternoon when I was washing my father's green and yellow 1954 Chevrolet, that I saw this young lady walking down Flood Street. I introduced myself to Vera L. Wright and told her after having made her acquaintance, "One day I am going to take you away from all of this." At that time we were in junior high school.

We seriously began dating in high school where I was one grade ahead of her. After high school I worked at the Charleston Naval Shipyard for about a year, and in July 1968 I enlisted in the United States Air Force. Before entering the military we had made plans to wed in January. When January

19, 1969 arrived Vera and I got married. Being on leave for a short while did not afford us the opportunity to have a big wedding so we were married at my pastor's parsonage.

That evening we both stood before the pastor and Almighty God and made a covenant of marriage. I remember we said to each other a phrase that has come back forty-five plus years for us to uphold: *In sickness and in health*. This was not a passing comment; not just ordinary words spoken in a moment of infatuation. We made a commitment to one another over the years to be there for each other. We had a few difficult days raising five children, but for the most part they were still alright. Our last son, David, was born pre-mature and that brought a new level of anxiety, but God delivered him and brought restoration. He is now twenty-seven years old and doing just fine by God's grace.

We have entered another season now in that Vera came down with an affliction, dementia. I perceive that this is a season ordained by God, and I trust Him to order our steps through this process. It appears quite easy to stand before the minister and say words. Yet, when difficulties hit your life, what do you do? Where do you go? How do you react to something that is not supposed to happen to you or your loved ones? As demanding and overwhelming an affliction may become, I have come to learn that God is always bigger than our problems. In Romans 8:28 the apostle Paul said, "And we know that all things work together for good to them that love the Lord; to those who are called according to His purpose."

When your life is not your own; when you have been bought with a price; when you are called to glorify God in your body; you have no choice but to cry out, "Lord, how am I going to handle this?" "What am I going to do?" Nothing happens to a believer in which God is unaware. There is no luck in the vocabulary of a child of God. Nevertheless, as I learn more about my wife's affliction, I said, "Lord, you know, and still I will trust you because I do not know what to do." These words we covenanted back on that Sunday evening in the pastor's parsonage came back to mind: *In sickness and in health*. Still I began to think back as to how and when this came upon her. My mind began to run to and fro, thinking, pondering, asking, praying and even pleading with God to take away this illness. God said, "Trust me. My grace is sufficient."

Vera was always quite independent, even though we did a lot of things together; she went anywhere and took care of herself and family business. However, I saw where familiar chores became a challenge for her. She had difficulty getting the car started. Simple things became a laborious task for her. I encouraged her to see someone about her memory. She replied that everything was fine and she did not see the need to consult a doctor. "Why should I have to go when things are alright with me?" she asked. So I would let it go for a while and would just observe. There were times she would forget things, and .SI asked the Lord, "How can I get her to see a clinician?" I prayed for Vera and asked the Lord to help her and bring restoration to her memory. No change. She finally gave up driving. It took a while but she eventually allowed me to make an appointment with our primary care physician.

The clinician saw her and did a thorough examination. She referred Vera to see the psychiatrist, thinking she may have been under stress. After a visit with the psychiatrist, I was called to the exam room and several questions were asked of my wife while I was present. Her answers seemed quite confusing. She talked about our children as if they were all still living in our home in Millbrook when only one of them is still living there. The psychiatrist recommended she be referred to see a neurologist. There was a concern that she may have had a stroke. I became more troubled yet told the clinician to make the referral appointment. I struggled to explain to Vera the results of this visit and the importance of seeing a neurologist. Vera was adamant that she had already seen the doctor and why should she have to see another. Finally, after much talking and explaining, she consented to see the referral doctor.

The neurologist examined Vera while I was also in the exam room, asking a series of questions and instructing her to perform several simple movements. One movement Vera was asked to do was touch her nose with her finger with her eyes closed. I noticed that she struggled to complete this task. After the neurologist made her assessment, she shared her initial findings. She scheduled Vera to see a clinician at the Sparks Clinic in Birmingham. She also ordered several laboratory tests and scheduled Vera for an MRI and EEG. Then the neurologist explained that once she would receive the results from these tests, she could provide a full diagnosis regarding Vera's condition.

December came rather quickly, and on the morning of her appointment in Birmingham it became a challenge. Vera objected to going to another appointment. I pleaded with her of the importance of this appointment. After much imploring, I retreated into the living room and laid it all out before the Lord, asking him to minister to my wife because I did not know what else to do. In her mind she did not see the need to go, but God spoke to her heart and she consented. Thank God for supplication. After this visit with the clinic personnel who assessed her cognitive abilities, they forwarded a report to her neurologist. It was determined that Vera had a mild dementia. This diagnosis came as a real shock to me. Upon hearing this report, I had so many questions. I began to become more in tune to any research or reports about dementia. I wanted to learn as much as I could about this disease to help me care for my wife the best way possible.

I remembered the Lord saying, "In everything give thanks for this is the will of God in Christ Jesus concerning you" (I Thessalonians 5:18). Additionally, the spirit of God brought to my mind again, "For we know that all things work together for good, for those who love God; for those who are the called according to His purpose" (Romans 8:28). Knowing that God will not bring things into our lives without a purpose, I began praying for strength and guidance concerning how I should handle this news. I sensed things would begin to change and would not be as it once was. I informed our children about the diagnosis so they would be aware of all that was happening. I did not keep anything from them and updated them often of their mother's status.

Vera and I have always faced things together, and I ask the Lord to give me what I need to make sure that she is taken care of. Regardless of how her condition may progress or digress, I am determined to serve her with all my heart. Aside from my Lord and Savior Jesus Christ, my wife has become the center stage in my life even the more, and I thank God for each day he has given us mutually to share with each other. Our covenant to one another *In sickness and in health* became more than just words. It became a reality. I am certain that God would meet our needs through this season. I am reminded that "It is of the Lord's mercies that we are not consumed, because his compassions fail not. They are new every morning; great is thy faithfulness" (Lamentations 3:22, 23).

As I reflect on this new period in our lives, I said to myself "if ever there was a time I need to rely on God's resources it is now." On that January evening in 1969, Vera and I recited many things that we intend to do as long as we both shall live *In sickness and in health* was one of those statements. The two shall become one flesh. As a result of our union, Vera and I became one. So whatever impacts Vera affects me and whatever impacts me affects her. Through the years we have always shared everything. Now we are presently going through the challenge of a health issue. God has kept us and will continue to supply our need according to His riches in glory by Jesus Christ. Let me share a verse of a song that Vera and I have come to appreciate because it speaks to where we are today. It is entitled, *Through the Years*, by Kenny Rogers:

> *Through the years, when everything went wrong*
> *Together we were strong, I know that I belonged*
> *right here with you*
> *Through the years I never had a doubt,*
> *We'd always worked things out*
> *I've learned what love's about, by loving you*
> *Through the years.*

In pondering over the period that God has brought and is taking us through, I am encouraged because I am reassured that He has it all under control. Nothing escapes His tender hands. In the case of God's servants, suffering is never pointless. It tests to strengthen or chastens to correct, after acting as a deterrent to sin. In the case of the apostle Paul it was an angel or messenger of Satan – perhaps some physical weakness or disability, but permitted by God. It was allowed by the permissible will of God (2 Corinthians 12:7-10). So as I view my wife's affliction with dementia, God has permitted it for a reason. It is teaching me that God's grace is sufficient.

In the role of caregiver, I rely upon all the resources He has brought to our attention. His Word is a source of comfort and guidance for me as I care for Vera and attend to her every need. Some days are better than others. No two days are the same. There are times of laughter and times of just wanting to get through the day. We have had a blessed 45 years of enjoying each other while in good health, and I intend with God's help to enjoy each day God gives to us during this period of sickness.

While I write these words Vera is standing by me serenading. Along with her serenading and my trying to listen to some light classical music, I reflect on how things once were for her. I remember how she was so vibrant and bubbly and how she once carried on very pointed conversations. Now our communication has been lessened due to the state of this disease. Often there are moments I get a reply from her that is on target and right on point to my question. There are times when a sparkle or glimmer of light comes through in her response. It is during those moments that I say thank you Lord and take pleasure in the response.

Therefore, as we walk this journey together, I am assured that God is with us. He has not taken away the burden of dementia from my wife and me, but He has granted me what I need to serve her. So as I gain strength from communing with Him I am able to assist Vera during this demanding and strenuous period in our lives. As I consider Scripture, the Lord brought this to mind, "Looking unto Jesus, the author and finisher of our faith; who for the joy that was set before him endured the cross, despising the shame, and is set down at the right hand of the throne of God" (Hebrews 12:2). As severe and ruthless a suffering he endured, surely He is able to succor me in aiding my wife during this chapter in our lives. *In sickness and in health* were covenant words we pledged to uphold, so I resolve to also fulfill this portion of our vows.

Chapter 4

GOD'S PENTAGON OF POTENCY

"Rejoice in the Lord always: and again I say rejoice."
(Philippians 4:4)

I thank God that for over forty-five years my life has been a faith walk. On December 15, 1968 I asked the Lord Jesus Christ to come into my life. That Sunday afternoon after Mack Crum shared the plan of salvation with me, my life was changed for all eternity. He advised me to memorize I John 5:11-12 and that he would pick me up for Bible study on Tuesday night. I committed to memorizing that verse and indeed he took me to a Bible study. There was a group of guys I met who were enthusiastic about the Christian life and showed their devotion to Jesus Christ by investing in men. I realized in that this setting I was on my way to being discipled.

This tract that God placed me on was very exciting. I never saw a bunch of guys so committed and sold out to the cause of Christ in this way. They ensured that I was being cared for as a babe in Christ. Soon after I came to Christ, I was taught how to have a personal "quiet time." This started for me a life of getting to know the Lord more and developing a closer walk with Him. Soon after coming to Christ, I returned home on leave and shared with Vera, and she gave her heart to Jesus. What a joy! We both started to walk in newness of life on this journey. We did not know what God had planned for us years later.

I was transferred to Randolph AFB, Texas four months later, and there I was under the guidance of Roger Witteveen. Roger was responsible for the guys at Randolph AFB. On Thursday night there would be approximately seventy to eighty men meeting for Bible study at a chapel on Fort Sam Houston. This was my time to continue growing in Christ. I learned a lot during my time in Texas. We would meet on Saturday mornings for prayer. Our spiritual leader's home would be the gathering site, and we met in one of the bed-rooms for prayer with just enough room to barely move about there were so many guys. What a precious and fruitful environment to be in as I was being mentored and encour-aged about the basics of the Christian life. Those were some great days of learning and being seasoned. I thank God for those He used to prepare me for where I am today. Nothing is wasted in the life of a believer, and I am grateful for the way God has ordered my steps. He has prepared Vera and me for this season. If it was not for God, I would not be writing this chapter.

Our great God and Savior did many things for us over the years. I praise God for his grace in keeping us. Now that we are both dealing with health issues, it is just like God to bring things to our remembrance. Just recently God showed me what I called "The Pentagon of His Potency." He led me to the book of Philippians. I had read this book many times before. However, this time it would be different. In this season of needing encouragement God showed me a five-fold connection.

First, I saw at the base of the pentagon, **praise**. In Philippians 4:4 it says, "Rejoice in the Lord always: and again I say, Rejoice." When one is dealing with afflictions, trials, and challenges in life, it is during these times that one should turn and give praise to God. The verse did not say sometimes or on occasion but always! God is certainly worthy of our praise. When we begin to praise God our focus changes from ourselves to God. During this season of affliction with cancer and being a caregiver for my wife, lifting my voice and heart in praise to God has been a blessing to me. I feel my deliverance and see the hand of God moving in so many ways. This brings to mind having read what Jehoshaphat did when he and Judah were facing an enemy much larger than they: "And Jehoshaphat feared and set himself to seek the Lord, and proclaimed a fast throughout all Judah" (II Chronicles 20:3). As a result of his prayer, the Spirit of the Lord spoke through Jahaziel; they were instructed to go toward the enemy early in the morning. Jehoshaphat and all Judah began worshipping the Lord. They were instructed to send singers in front of the army that they should praise the beauty of holiness. As they went before the army they were to say, Praise the Lord; for his mercy endureth forever. And when they began to sing and to praise, the Lord set ambushments against the children of Ammon, Moab, and mount Seir, they were smitten. They were abundantly blessed with riches and precious jewels that took three days to collect it was so much" (II Chronicles 20:14a, 16, 20-22, 25). The point is that God appreciates our praise. He is the center and focus of our praise.

When I turned my attention and focus upon God, I began to see His hand at work in our season and moving hearts to respond to our need. There is something about praising God that takes away the weight of the affliction. The problem was not removed, but He granted me grace and mercy to endure. I praise God for His goodness and grace which are inexhaustible. Paul and Silas knew it too well as they were imprisoned in Philippi. The Scriptures share how they prayed and sang praises to God from their jail cell. God caused the very foundations of the prison to be shaken and everyone's shackles were unfastened. The jailor was about to kill himself thinking that the prisoners had escaped. However, Paul shouted, "Do not harm yourself because no one had escaped!" The jailor in turn asked Paul and Silas, "What is necessary for me to do that I may be saved?" And they answered, "Believe in the Lord Jesus Christ and you will be saved, you and your household." Thus, Paul and Silas declared the Word of God to the jailor and all who were in his house. Wow! These men of God did not complain because of their situation but they sang praises to Almighty God (Acts 16). Yes, there is some-thing about praising God that calms our fears. God honors praise. "I will bless the Lord at all times: his praise shall con-tinually be in my mouth" (Psalm 34:1). Lord, no matter what happens, may your praise proceed from my heart to my lips. I worship your magnificence!

Secondly, as I viewed the pentagon on the left, I saw **prayer**. Philippians 4:6 states, "Be careful for nothing; but in everything by prayer and supplication with thanksgiving let your requests be made known unto God" (Phil. 4:6). I real-ized the importance of prayer, for indeed it is how we com-municate and talk with God. The direction is twofold: don't worry about anything and pray about everything in a spirit of thanksgiving and gratefulness. As I consider my affliction of cancer and also Vera's dementia, I find myself praying more often. I turned the controls over to the Lord Who alone is sov-ereign and is engineering our lives because He knows what we need. There is no limit to God. We have human limitations but God does not. Even during this season I am instructed to "give thanks for this is the will of God in Christ Jesus con-cerning me" (I Thessalonians 5:18). Therefore, I examine the situation and let the Lord handle the control. I am reminded of a song entitled "Living for Jesus". One of the verses says: "Living for Jesus a life that is true, striving to please Him in all that I do, Yielding allegiance, glad-hearted and free. This is the pathway of blessing for me." Yes, even as I experience the ups and downs of this affliction and the changes associ-ated with being a caregiver, it is still the pathway of blessing.

God does not waste anything. I remember one of my pastors, Jack Spears, saying, "God can even use our sin to benefit us." So I choose to devote myself to praying and spending time with God.

While assigned in Southeast Asia in the early seventies, I attended a servicemen conference and recalled a speaker, Paul Kelley, speaking on "Quiet Time." He stated the importance of getting that time with God. It was absolutely necessary for one's growth. Oswald Chambers said, "Spend plenty of time with God; let other things go, but don't neglect Him." Oh, how I see the truth of those statements and the importance of meeting with God and conversing with Him each day. This side of God's pentagon of potency is vital and critical to the believer. It is just as necessary as food and water is to the body that one spends time in prayer and supplication with God. Any great conquest one undertakes must be bathed in prayer. Thus, because of the challenge that God has allowed to come my way, it is imperative that I seek Him and "cast all my care upon Him because He cares for me" (I Peter 5:7). David reminds us "many are the afflictions of the righteous; but the Lord delivers him out of them all" (Psalm 34:19).

It is a comfort to my heart to know that the God that we serve hears our prayers. The Psalmist states, "Evening, and morning, and at noon, will I pray, and cry aloud; and he shall hear my voice" (Psalm 55:17). Therefore, we can go to God at any time, let our requests be made known, and let Him know what is on our heart. It should be a time of adoration, confession, thanksgiving and supplication. My time of getting with God is early in the morning. Things are quiet, and I can meditate upon the Word and pray out aloud to Him. On occasion when Vera is still asleep, I may take my thirty minute walk. It is breathtaking when the sun comes up over the tree tops. I am walking and communing with God. Then as I sit in the living room where I have my devotional time, I open the blinds and am able to view the sunrise as well. It is a beautiful sight to behold. When I have a "tearful eye moment," believe me I have lots of those, especially as I look at the love of my life slowly declining, I usually pause and reflect on the awesome view of the heavens. The songwriter said it so well, and I write in part: "In the stars his handiwork I see; on the wind he speaks with majesty....what is that to me? "The heavens declare the glory of God; the firmament shows his handiwork" (Psalm 19:1). The next time you are going through a rough time, pause, step outside in the evening and view God's amazing creation. It is so vast, and the heavens are limitless. It is our God who looks forward to having time with us in prayer. I could spend hours on the prayer side of the pentagon of God's potency, but there are three more to discuss. Prayer is an awesome thing!

Now let me view the pentagon from the right. Here I see *peace*. Philippians 4:7 states, "And the peace of God, which passeth all understanding, shall keep your hearts and minds through Christ Jesus." It transcends or surpasses all comprehending. It enables me to maintain my focus. Words that come to mind when I think of peace are calm, quiet, and silence. Sometimes we experience the storms of life, and things seem to be raging out of control. We are not able to handle the oars as we struggle to keep the boat afloat. Yet, the Spirit of God begins to move upon us as we call unto God, and He answers just like He did over 2,000 years ago when Jesus was in the boat with the disciples. He was asleep when they came upon a raging storm in the midst of the Sea of Galilee. They immediately called out to Jesus and awoke him out of sleep. Jesus arose, rebuked the wind, and said unto the sea, "Peace, be still!" Then Jesus instructed the disciples, "Let us go over to the other side." (Mark 4:35-39). When we are led by the Spirit of God and when we are told by the Lord to move in a certain direction, to go to a particular place, to speak for Him, whatever the situation is, if we are in the center of God's will, that is the best place to be. In spite of the storms of life which will come, we are in the Master's hand, and nothing can overtake us without His permission.

The disciples learned a valuable lesson that day on the Sea of Galilee. So it is with you and me. There will be life crises that we must endure, yet God has promised His peace. There is no better calm and quiet than that which is produced by our loving Savior. He spoke peace to me when I became the caregiver for Vera. It seemed like a hail storm hit when we received her diagnosis of dementia. I cried unto the Lord about her affliction. However, the Lord quieted my spirit, spoke to my heart, and reassured me once again that He is in control, that Vera belonged to Him. So for a season of several years now He allowed me to adjust to being a caregiver. There are times I would have my moments of sadness and would have to remind myself and encourage myself with God's Word. Therefore, I needed to get on with the challenge of living and taking care of her. God will provide. His peace does transcend all understanding. When the world says, "Brother, I don't know if I could do what you are doing," God places such peace in my heart and soul, and I dare not move from the place where He has positioned me. Being in the center of God's will is the place of blessing. The storms may still be raging, and the ups and downs of being a caregiver are real, but God says to my stormy seasons, "Peace, be still!" When He speaks, the situation must do what He says. Wow! The Creator of all things speaks on my behalf and because He is sovereign, the situation, the sickness, the storms of life must bow to His command. So I just praise God for His peace. The God of peace grants to us His peace. Jesus said, "These things I have spoken unto you, that in me ye might have peace. In the world ye shall have tribulation: but be of good cheer; I have overcome the world" (John 16:33).

Hence, this side of the pentagon is looking, as my pastor would say, "wonderful" and very fitting for me to appropriate as I go forward. One can count it all joy when the Lord is with him in the midst of the storms of life and when one experiences the peace of God in his soul. It is like the Hebrew writer explained, "For the word of God is quick and powerful [living and operative], and sharper than any two-edged sword, piercing even to the dividing of soul and spirit, and of the joints and marrow, and is a discerner of the thoughts and intents of the heart" (Hebrews 4:12). When I think of how deep the Word of God penetrates one's life, I am amazed. Medically, the bone marrow is about as far as one can go into the skeleton of the body. God speaks peace to my innermost being. Yes, I still have the everyday challenges, but I have committed them unto my Lord and He is taking care of Vera and me. I thank God for His perfect peace as I keep my mind stayed upon Him. Let me encourage you my friends to allow the peace of God to rule in your hearts.

I have learned that peace is one of the nine graces. It is part of the nine that is produced by the Spirit. Peace along with love and joy produces character as an inward state. Therefore, as I yield myself to Him, I can experience the peace of God from the God of peace. When the storms keep on raging without, I have peace within because He is my anchor. He is my pillow so I can rest my head upon His breast and be at peace. Come what may, as a believer, I belong to Him and whatever He allows has sifted through His mighty yet tender hands. So the world is puzzled when the believer can rejoice and be still in the midst of a crisis. My church has a saying, "When Christ is center, crises cease." So I keep pressing and commit the day to my great God who alone is sovereign and can handle each one of my situations. He says, "Peace, be still!"

I will at this time turn my attention to the top right segment of this pentagon of God's potency. Here I discover God's *power*. He further says," I can do all things through Christ which strengthened me" (Philippians 4:13). One of the attributes of God is that He is omnipotent: almighty, all-powerful, invincible. When Jesus came out of the grave before He ascended He told the disciples, "...all power is given unto me in heaven and in earth" (Matthew 28:18). Christ has all authority and dominion. Everything is subject unto Him. One of the resources that God has made available to believers is His strength. I can never accomplish anything of lasting value when done in the flesh. However, when I commit myself to Christ and abide in His will for my life, it is unlimited what He can do in and through my life. Consequently, when you or I are dealing with problems or confronted with trials, we can rely upon His strength to enable us to withstand these matters. I am reminded what the prophet Isaiah said regarding God's strength and power: "Fear thou not; for I am with thee; be not dismayed; for I am thy God; I will strengthen thee; yea, I will keep thee; yea, I will uphold thee with the right hand of my righteousness" (Isaiah 41:10). I assuredly and without a doubt can testify of God's strength and power. When undergoing chemotherapy, I began to feel very weak. I still tried to take care of Vera. I was thankful for Elaine Parks, a home health nurse, who availed herself to serve Vera while I was going through treatment. She was a Godsend and stood in the gap for us.

I recall how the Lord allowed me to adjust to caring for her. After a while, I developed a system to assist her in getting ready for the day. However, as I was dealing with treatments, I felt myself getting weaker. What normally would take about 10 minutes lasted for nearly a half hour or longer. I would have to take breaks and sit for a bit while I catch my breath. Leaning over became a chore. I cried unto the Lord and said, "I need your help to get through this season; it is very hard. I cannot do this and deal with my own issues too!" Yet, He reminded me that His grace was sufficient. As I turned and focused upon Him, I was able to continue. I had to lean upon Him. The Lord sent others along to help. I know the saints were praying for us, and I could feel the impact of their prayers. God was sustaining us and upholding us as the saints interceded on our behalf.

Throughout the course of being treated, my laboratory results were declining, and I felt the changes as I began to get weaker. However, I would continue, quoting: "I can do all things through Christ who strengthens me." I walked into therapy each Monday and daily into radiation for 40 days, sometimes a bit slower but steady moving forward. I know God's power was available for me to tap into. I observed others who were being treated there also. Many were carried in with the help of a loved one or using a wheel chair or other devices, yet the Lord allowed me to walk in each day and walk out on my own. Other than Mondays when Pad would drive me and bring me back home, I would drive myself the other four days of the week for radiation treatment. "Lord," I would pray, "grant me strength to get through this day." He gave me a measure of strength to endure each day. Toward the end of chemotherapy my red blood cell count was very low. This accounted for why I felt so weak. The hematology oncologist ordered a blood transfusion. Now, you must know that for better part of my secular career I worked in the blood bank section of the clinical laboratory and processed many units of blood for patients. Now it was time for me to submit to getting two units of blood. I walked tenderly and slowly into Jackson Hospital on that morning. The staff was very professional and proficient. Medical people, as I was, can be difficult patients at times, but I submitted myself to these skilled practitioners and did not complain. After a few hours of receiving two units of blood I felt like I was walking on clouds. I felt stronger. The tiredness and lightheadedness I felt earlier had subsided. God was working through the medical treatment to bring strength back to me.

Sometimes you feel as if you cannot take another step due to the challenges of daily living. Nevertheless, God is always there to strengthen, keep and uphold you. I have come to realize more and more what the apostle Paul was saying about God's power. Yes, I can do all things through Christ who strengthens me. When one is walking uprightly and along the path that God has ordained, he or she can be satisfied and appreciate the unlimited potential one has because of the Lord Jesus Christ. God did say that "He will not withhold any good thing from those who walk uprightly" (Psalm 89:1). I pray to continue to honor the Lord through obedient and faithful living.

This pentagon of God's potency is shaping up. I will now turn my attention to the fifth and final section of the pentagon. Here God showed me His **provision**. Philippians 4:19 states, "But my God shall supply all your need according to his riches in glory by Christ Jesus." The apostle Paul responded about his gratitude for what he had received. Then he encouraged the saints at Philippi that God will meet their need. Oh how this blesses my soul! When I trust God with whatever He has placed into my hands, He can do much more with it than I can. For example, in the area of finances, I have learned that He needs to be Lord of everything in my life. This is a lesson Vera and I discovered a long time ago at Shawview Presbyterian Church. It was there that we were taught the importance of tithing. We learned a lot of principles during those early days in our Christian lives. Also in the area of marriage, God provided sound instructions for us. Vera attended a class on the Gracious Woman and I attended one on the Challenge to Christian Manhood. We realized that we were deficient in many areas of understanding what God required. However, we were willing to commit ourselves to receive further instructions in these areas. We prayed for wisdom to handle God's resources in a fruitful way. Everything of everything belongs to God.

God's provision also brings to mind that Jesus is our Shepherd, and we have no need to lack. He makes us lie down in *green* pastures and beside waters of *quietness*. He restores our soul and leads us onto paths of righteousness. We are His sheep and are in constant need of His providing for He knows what is best for the sheep. As our trusted Shepherd, He provides protection for the flock in a loving manner. He is the God of all comfort. His presence offers comfort. There are times when gloom may cast a shadow on our day, yet as believers we can abide in His presence and all gloominess and despair subsides.

A sheep needs daily pasture and the shepherd is tasked to locate provision for his sheep's daily needs. God's provision for my family is just awesome. In 1972 when our third child, Patrick, came along, Vera and I prayed about whether she should remain working as an LPN or remain at home with our three children, Carmela, Paul and now Patrick. Therefore, after much prayer, we decided she would stop working and remain at home with our children. God never allowed us to miss a meal; He provided for us. Vera's choice to be at home was the best decision and a wise one. Those kids really looked forward to their mom being at home when they arrived from school. She was available to cater to their being involved in activities, and together we saw the hand of God moving through our family. Today, "I have no greater joy than to hear that my children walk in truth" (III John 4). We became a one income family, but in spite of that, the God that we serve is Jehovah-jireh. The name translated as "The Lord Will Provide." This name was mentioned in Genesis 22:14 when God provided a ram for Abraham to sacrifice instead of his son, Isaac. Our cupboard was never empty as we trusted God with all that we had. We kept back nothing, and God made provision for us. That was over forty years ago. Thus far God has and continues to meet all our needs.

We experience His immutability. He is the same yesterday, today and forever. Four years ago my supervisor and regional manager came into my office and advised me that due to financial reasons they needed to take my position. In other words, I was let go from my position as supervisor of the clinical laboratory. I was not given the customary two-week notice; it was time for me to vacate this employment. I requested a few more hours for me to clear out my office and make some needed communications. I called Vera and told her I will be coming home for lunch permanently! There was no struggle or anxiety with this sudden change. I rejoiced in knowing that my God is able to provide, and that He did. I just knew and still know that when God is Lord of your life, those events had already sifted through His tender loving hands. God engineered what takes place in my life, and I was called to be faithful and obedient.

I had just contracted during this time with a publisher to produce our first book, <u>Building A Strong Christian Family</u>. A lot of things became more focused. The last chapter I was writing was entitled: "In sickness and in health." God was waiting for me to write this chapter because He needed me to be at home with my wife. Don't tell me! I serve a great, awesome God and nothing takes Him by surprise! I left the workplace four years ago and to God be the glory I never retreated. I saw the need to become my wife's primary care-giver, and I serve her with honor, remembering our covenant: "in sickness and in health." God did not let us skip a beat. We made some adjustments financially, but we kept pressing forward. God never allowed the barrel of meal to fail. He constantly provides.

I contemplated resigning from my board position with the American Medical Technologist, but my children encouraged me to stay connected in that I needed the professional association. They said, "Dad whenever you have to attend a board meeting, we will come and stay with Mom." My board meetings were normally a 3-4 day trip, and they were willing to stand in the gap for their mother and me. Wow! She was always there for them, and now they wanted to be there for her, and to this day they have consistently come home when they are able to be with us. They call often to check on us and inquire time and again as to whether we needed anything. That is God's provision, my friends, at its best. Their response gives me joy unspeakable. That is why I can count it all joy.

Over this past year as I underwent the ups and downs of cancer, God continued to show Himself strong on our behalf and moved upon the body of Christ to supply our every need. A large quantity of prayers was being made for us. We never missed a meal. Tangible financial needs were met and provided. Others came and sat with Vera. There were plenty of calls and inquiries. I had to learn to be a recipient of God's goodness and provision as He moved on the hearts of so many to respond. This season, my friends, has not been trouble-free, but God has taken away the anxiety and said, "I got this." So I am able to "Keep Pressing" and allow Him to use every trial for the praise of His glory.

Before I close this chapter, I am reminded of the ultimate provision. The apostle Paul said, "He that spared not his own Son, but delivered him up for us all, how shall he not with him also freely give us all things" (Romans 8:32). The paragraph begins with God saying through Paul, "And we know that all things work together for good to them that love God, to them who are the called according to his purpose" (Romans 8:28). God purposed that Vera and I would experience this trial and that He would provide for our every need. Jesus paid our sin debt in full. Our spiritual and physical healing is centered in Jesus, and all to Him we owe! Our greatest need was fulfilled in the person of our Lord Jesus Christ who went to Calvary's cross for our sins. The zenith of all that we would ever need is found in our Lord and Savior Jesus Christ. "Therefore we do not lose heart, but though our outer man is decaying, yet our inner man is renewed day by day. For momentary, light affliction is producing for us an eternal weight of glory far beyond all comprehension, while we do not look at the things which are seen, but at the things which are not seen; for the things which are seen are temporal, but the things which are not seen are eternal" (II Corinthians 4:16-18, NAS). My friends let me encourage you to trust in God who is able to provide and meet every need superabundantly!

GOD'S PENTAGON OF POTENCY

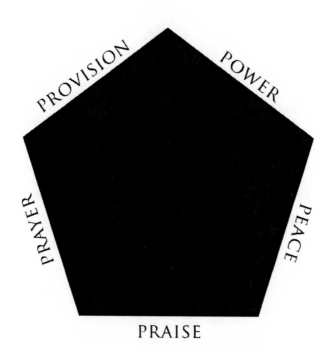

Chapter 5

IT IS JUST A SEASON

"To everything there is a season, and a time for every purpose under the heaven." (Ecclesiastes 3:1)

Every season has specific qualities that describe or set it apart from the others. As I think about the four seasons: winter, spring, summer and fall (autumn), my favorite is autumn. The weather is mild, and the leaves begin to change a beautiful orange, reddish, yellow, brown; it is just breathtaking. I say to myself that I can have this experience year round. On the other hand the seasons are set by God, and we all have to go through each one. We will be subjected to the ice and cold temperatures of winter, the allergy flare-ups that spring brings with the release of pollen, and the heat of summer that pushes one to drink more water. Yet, there are good things within each of the four seasons.

Just as there are four seasons through which the earth rotates, there are also seasons of life that we must go through.

The Scriptures state, "To everything there is a season, and a time to every purpose under the heaven" (Ecclesiastes 3:1). Just like the four annual seasons last for a certain time, there are seasons in our lives that come and go. As I look back over our lives I can see God's hand at work leading and guiding us. To date, Vera and I have experienced 45 plus years of marriage. God has blessed us to raise five children from infancy, through adolescence, and on to adulthood. Each one of them is different and came with their own package of characteristics.

God gave us wisdom to raise up a godly seed, and "I have no greater joy to know that each one of them [all five] are walking in truth" (III John 4). We dealt with the challenges of their infancy with the changing of diapers, feeding with bottles, and keeping them clean to adolescence and their seeking to do for themselves and making their mark. Then we faced their teenage years with curfews, dating, and independence. You name it. We had experienced it. However, through it all, they came out alright. Proverbs 22:6 says, "Train up a child in the way he should go; and when he is old, he will not depart from it." Each one of them is involved in some aspect of serving Christ.

The same is true when we acquire an affliction. Wisdom from God needs to be employed. Vera having been diagnosed with dementia was a new season for us to go through. God has allowed this affliction to filter through His hands and orchestrated it so that I would be her primary caregiver. Vera and I made a pledge to one another: "In sickness and in health" to stay together. This season had arrived for me to be there for her.

These last several years have seemed rather long. To observe your loved one of 45 years decline has been extremely difficult. I pray for daily grace and strength to perform my duties of a caregiver with joy. There are times when I get tired, realizing that my wife's responses are due in part or whole to her dementia. Yet, I recognize her as my queen and will cater to her every need.

Just as the leaves change color in autumn, I see the changes in Vera that surfaced due to her dementia such as her ability to remember her family and fond memories. In spite of the disease, she still gives the beautiful smile that I have come to love over these many years. As she naps, sometime she will verbalize. Then I ask myself, "I wonder what she is saying?". She will then awaken, sit up, and look at me. Then I would say, "I was looking at you while you were taking a nap." She would smile and dose off to nap a little more.

The music on the radio is soothing. So I listen as I journal and reflect on God's goodness during this season. I prayed, "I thank you God for this 'autumn' experience of change. Give me wisdom and strength, Lord, to adapt and adjust to the daily changes as they show forth themselves. It is only a season; however, I wonder how long!"

Furthermore, I count it all joy as Vera and I take this journey together, during this season that was ordained of God. "And we know that all things work together for good to them that love God; to them who are the called according to His purpose" (Romans 8:28).

The apostle James reminds me "But let patience have her perfect work that ye may be perfect and entire, wanting nothing" (James 1:4). In other words, whatever test one undergoes, do not try to get out of it ahead of time or impulsively. There is a purpose concerning the testing of our faith. We should let it do its work.

I was encouraged by a recent devotional that focused on the point that God is not finished with you. Life is lived in seasons. If you do not understand that, you will be constantly frustrated. The farmer knows the best time for planting, so he will place his seeds in the ground. Then he must pause and allow time for the seeds to take root downward. After a season of delay it is followed by a bountiful harvest. The time varies with each test or season. One may get impatient and feel discouraged with the length of time it is taking for change to occur, but the great God that we serve is patient and never in a panic, even if we are in a frenzy. God is orchestrating and engineering our lives so He sets the standard and timetable.

As I consider and meditate on the fact that God has everything under control, it brought peace to my soul. All of it is working for my good. I perceived that there is no bad season. Changes? Yes! However, God showed me that in every season He takes me through there are valuable lessons to be learned and nuggets of truth to appropriate. The everyday ups and downs that accompany life's issues are not designed to cause one shipwreck but are to the praise of His glory. I won't always be in rough waters; however, the experience of any season is designed to take me to a higher level.

In that, "to everything there is a season," I long for all that God has for me. You, my dear friend, should desire God's best. All the more so when the storm clouds of life arise, God can still use it to His glory; "As the tender grass springing out of the earth by clear shining after rain," (II Samuel 3:4-6). So a believer can benefit from the storms of life.

The apostle Paul instructs us, "In everything give thanks; for this is the will of God in Christ Jesus concerning you" (I Thessalonians 5:18). No matter what the circumstances may be or the seasons I might experience, I am to be thankful and give thanks. Jesus Christ is the Revealer and Mediator of that will. So abiding in the center of God's will is the best place for me.

When one's life is fully surrendered to God, submission to the divine will of God will produce what God desires for us. Through the seasons of life God has a plan to give us a future and a hope. It is my desire to stand perfect and complete, firm and mature in all the will of God. Therefore, we give God thanks for every season of life. God knows no limit!

Chapter 6

COUNT IT ALL JOY

*"My brethren, count it all joy when ye fall into divers
temptations." (James 1:2)*

"*C*ount it all joy." Years ago this phrase used to be my
signature comment when departing or closing a
letter. The phrase is easy to say. Until now, it had been a
farewell phrase. To tell someone "See you later," I would say,
"Count it all joy."

It was meant to be an encouragement to whoever I was
speaking to, urging them to keep moving forward. Fittingly
on two separate occasions a very dear friend of mine asked
me if I was counting it all joy. The first time was when Vera
was diagnosed with dementia. He asked, "Hey, Paul, are you
counting it all joy?" I understood what he was asking, and
indeed it was hard to say, "Yes, I am." His inquiry was not to
get at me but to remind me that in spite of the situation I
can *count it all joy*. On the second occasion it was after I was

told that I had a malignant salivary tumor. "Hey, Paul, are you counting it all joy?" He asked. I felt so hurt because of the diagnosis, but a true friend would inquire to make sure that you are doing alright. His purpose was to strike a chord with me in my situation, to remind me that I can still count it all joy in the midst of this difficult season. Vera and I are experiencing a most trying time in our lives, and it is pleasing when someone genuinely wants to know how you are.

Chapters 1 and 2 of the book of James concentrate on the testing of one's faith. Specifically, verses 1-12 of chapter one centers on the purpose of testing's. Clearly, as I look at the Scripture in context, here is what James 1:2 says, "*My brethren, count it all joy when ye fall into divers temptation.*" The Greek word for joy in this verse is *chara*, in which it has a noun meaning joy or delight. I see this joy as connected with falling into trials. Consequently, being a caregiver and now having my own affliction are like a double blow. I called it "strike two." As a result, I am reminded that trials and afflictions are designed to strengthen my faith. So then living faith is tested by trials.

Furthermore the testing of my faith will produce fortitude. In other words I will become resilient. This in turn has led me to rely upon God's resources and allow the Lord to be in control of my life. God has shown himself to be strong on our behalf, and I am certain that He will do the same for us as we go through this phase.

This brings to mind a time when my family and I were going to Charleston, South Carolina, during the Christmas season. We just crossed into Georgia when I heard a noise. I stopped the car and began to check the tires and did not find anything wrong. So returning to driving I still hears this noise. I told the family, "I do not know what it is, but we had better turn around, return home and get the other car." We did not want to get out into middle Georgia and suffer a breakdown. We turned around and just after we crossed back into Alabama the noise got louder. Soon afterwards the car came to an abrupt stop. It felt like we had run over a log in the road, which we did not. The car would no longer move forward or reverse. I perceived that we had transmission problems. There we were on Christmas Eve with a car full of presents and luggage, trying to decide what to do. We were a little over an hour away from home. I called one of the deacons of the church who came and picked us up. We left the van on the side of the road. Deacon Walker took us home. It was late, and I was in no mood to pack up another car so we stayed home for Christmas. The kids were upset, but we had no choice. I was thankful we were able to return home. The day after Christmas we went to check on getting the van towed to a nearby town for repair. Upon approaching to the van we noticed from a distance it looked different. Upon coming closer we realized that the entire driver side was sideswiped. After getting the van towed and with counsel from the insurance company, the van was totaled. I did not rejoice and was not a happy camper; yet, God kept us from further harm. Did I count it all joy? Not right then, but I knew that this situation and test were going to work for our good.

We ended up getting a new van Yes, we had to make payments for a while, but I thank God for keeping us safe. That was twelve years ago, and we are still driving that same van.

We all are going to experience the storms of life. The rain falls on the just and the unjust, so being a believer does not exempt one from the trials of life. The verse says to count it all joy *"when"* you fall into divers temptations. It will be a matter of time when each of us will encounter various trials in our lives. James instructs us to be joyful. I can hear someone who is not of faith saying, "Man, if that was me, bump it." Conversely, one should not listen to just any counsel, but only that which will edify and provide sound guidance. God uses the Scriptures to provide that guidance through one's personal time with Him or through others who are concerned about one's spiritual welfare. We should earnestly seek this guidance to help us be joyful during times of trial or affliction.

I recalled going through hurricanes that would strike my home city when I was young. It was seasonal, but the hurricane was no respecter of persons. My family and I lived in city housing and did not have a storm cellar or transportation to go anywhere. So we had to weather the storm. Some of them were quite severe and produced a lot of damage, but we made it through. The challenge afterwards was to pick up the pieces and recover. Then there were some marks which remain as evidence that a storm had passed by. Accordingly, when life throws various storms our way, we should not allow them to keep us down. Yes, there will be some marks that show we have experienced a test or trial, but we can begin again. Just like the recovery period and putting things back in place after a hurricane and the like, one can put things back into place in ones' life. As the songwriter, Larnelle Harris, said "[You can do it] with the passion of a child; you can begin again."

I am reminded of the patriarchs of old. Seemingly each one of them faced some test or underwent a contest; yet, they relied upon Almighty God to order their steps and direct their paths. None of them had it "easy." Jesus said, "These things I have spoken unto you, that in me ye might have peace. In the world ye might have tribulation: but be of good cheer; I have overcome the world" (John 16:33). He did not say that we will have tribulation all the time. He stated ye might have tribulation. And so when the trials of life or a storm come our way, we can rely upon our God who is able to strengthen, help and uphold us with his righteous right hand. Bear in mind that it was Jesus who said "Peace, be still." It was Jesus who "created all things and by him all things consists or holds together." It was Jesus who said, "Before Abraham was, I am." It was Jesus who said, "I and the father are one." So my dear friend, we have all authority at our disposal and by relying upon His strength we can weather any storm and may very well rejoice in the midst of the storms of life.

I can count it all joy! Count the suffering as joy; count the affliction as joy; and count the ups and downs of the Christian life as joy! We "look unto Jesus, the author and finisher of our faith; who for the *joy* that was set before him endured the cross, despising the shame and is set down at the right hand of the throne of God" (Hebrews 12:2). When I consider what Jesus went through for me and what He has done for me, my thoughts regarding my affliction cannot compare to the suffering he endured. Yet it was joy to Him to suffer in our place. So *when* we encounter the trials of life, we too can be joyful. It may not seem natural to the world that one would be singing in the midst of a storm; yet, Jesus was sleeping during the storm. I said earlier that we have a saying at Sanctuary that says, "When Christ is center, crises cease." He too was in the boat with the disciples. In the heart of the raging wind and waves, He was fast asleep. We too can rest in his care when we encounter any trial. He spoke to the elements, and they obeyed; Jesus can also speak to your situation and mine. I have learned to make sure that He is in the equation of my life and decision-making.

For that reason I can run to the Rock that is higher than I. David said it this way, "God is my refuge and strength, a very present help in trouble. Therefore will not we fear though the earth be removed, and though the mountains be carried into the midst of the sea; Though the waters thereof roar and be troubled, though the mountains shake with swelling thereof" (Psalm 46:1-3). I can count it all joy knowing that all of heaven is on hand to help out and provide support for me.

My grandson, Lil Em, and I were leaving the bowling alley one day. I commented on how beautiful and sunny the day is becoming. He stated, "Every weekend is like today, but it always rains a lot during the weekdays." Reflecting on his reply, I thought to myself, that the trials of life are similar to the weather. Each day is different and has its own challenges and blessings. I count it all joy as I encounter the day's ups and downs. Each day is the day that The Lord hath made; so I will rejoice and be glad in it.

I told the Lord in March 1971, that my life is completely at his disposal. So this season of affliction being ordained of God is a cause to count as joy. This trial is a testimony to my Lord and Savior. The Lord healed me spiritually on December 15, 1968 when Christ came into my life. Forty-five years later I was diagnosed with cancer; today six months after treatment, it is in remission. I perceive the Lord allowed me to experience this affliction so I may testify of His goodness and grace; it has given me another platform from where I may give testimony of God's physical healing.

I remember how He fed the multitudes and instructed the twelve disciples to collect the leftovers. They collected twelve baskets full. I suggest this as a testimony to the disciples of what Jesus was able to do with little when given to Him in his hands. So I gave this cancer to God to handle, and I count it all joy what God has done through this process. My life belongs to Jesus. It is not my own. I pray to glorify God in this earth suit, that all praise and honor and glory will go to Him and to Him alone!

In James's writings to the Christian Jews of the Dispersion, he shares for fifty-three verses in the first two chapters, the focus being the testing of faith. His theme appears to have been religion, the Greek meaning *threskeia,* "outward religious service" as the expression and proof of faith. Yet, in the very beginning of chapter one he calls attention for the believer to express joy when he or she undergoes what I call the *PAST*: Persecutions, Afflictions, Sufferings and Trials. Endurance when under trials proves our faith, even more so when we can count it all joy. Joy in suffering does not make sense from a worldly perspective. Nonetheless, as a child of God we are not of this world; we are in it but not of it. So as we are taught many principles in Christianity to employ, we must be taught how to respond *when* we are hit with *PAST*.

Count It All Joy! As I reflect further on this phrase, I feel constrained to look deeper. The Greek word for *count* is (*Hegeomai*), primarily, to lead the way; hence, to lead before the mind. I am to give much thought to what the situation is before me, in this case, an affliction. Keeping this thought in mind, I recall Douglas Miller's song, "Unspeakable Joy." When one thinks of the goodness of the Lord, in spite of the circumstances, joy should overflow our hearts. Unspeakable, undefinable, inexpressible, beyond words, this joy that I have found, the world did not give it and the world cannot take it away. I too get overwhelmed as I reflect on what God is doing in and through my life with this season of affliction; yet, I got joy!

This joy is another one of the nine graces the apostle Paul spoke about in Galatians 5:22-23. The presence of the Holy Spirit produces joy (gladness) in the heart. It is an inward state of character and I praise God that I am able to rejoice in the midst of anything. It makes one want to burst out in shout and praise to God. I found myself many times singing and thanking God even when things are rather tough.

Chapter 7

STILL I WILL TRUST YOU

"Though he slay me, yet will I trust in him: but I will maintain mine own ways before him." (Job 13:15)

Life throws at you ups and downs, thrills and trials, joy and sadness, wealth and poverty, sickness and health, and the list just continues on and on. As I journey through this land, I have experience a reasonable share of many of these contrasts. As a result, I have concluded that I must place my trust in God. He alone is all-knowing, all-wise, all-powerful, everywhere-present, unchanging, and cannot lie! This is the God I serve. I would like for you to pay close attention to these words:

> *STILL I WILL TRUST YOU*
> *I've climbed a mountain*
> *I've walked a valley low;*
> *And there's a hand, guiding me*
> *Where to go.*

So I cannot question,
When storm clouds come my way;
For I have placed my trust in You,
And You alone.

Still I will trust you,
Still I will follow,
Still I will listen to your every calling;
While the storm rages on
And I can't find my way,
Still I will trust you Lord.

When in my dark hour
You restored my weary soul,
You led me to that resting place
And made me whole.
So I cannot question
When stormy billows roll,
My faith is secure
Safe in my trust in you alone.

Still I will trust you
Still I will follow
Still I will listen to your every calling
While the storm rages on
And I can't find my way
Still I will trust you Lord.
(Adapted from Brooklyn Tabernacle-Favorite Song of All)

Wow! Isn't that amazing? Once again we all will encounter life's trials, but we can still trust God with every one of them. David reminds me that "The Lord is my Shepherd; I shall not want. He maketh me to lie down in green pastures: he leadeth me besides *still* waters" (Psalm 23:1-2). "Still" waters or quiet waters make known to me that I should be "still" as I place my trust in God alone. Moses instructed the Israelites to "Fear ye not, stand *still* and see the salvation of The Lord which he will show to you today: for the Egyptians whom ye have seen today, ye shall see them again no more forever" (Exodus 14:13).

Let me take you to the New Testament in Luke chapter 10 when Mary was sitting quietly at Jesus' feet. Martha was busy making preparation for dinner, but Mary sought to spend time with Jesus. It is not that what Martha was doing was not acceptable, but there is a time we need to be still and listen to what God has to say. Lord, still I will trust You!

Job, an early patriarch, had his share of troubles. I coined the phrase: "Job had a 4.0 GPA with God." The Scripture tells us "and that man was perfect and upright, one that feared God and eschewed evil" (Job 1:1). In spite of his acceptable testimony before God, trouble came knocking on Job's door. With the loss of children, property, good health and unwise counsel from his wife, he made this profound conclusion: "Though he slay me, yet will I trust in him" (Job 13:15a). What a testimony amidst all that he was experiencing. He walked uprightly before God, was a man of faith and prayer, and continued to maintain his integrity and trust in God. That is a powerful testimony. "Still I will trust you, Lord!"

It is a matter of absolute trust. I believe Abraham would agree with that statement. God promised Abraham that he will have a son; that his seed would be numerous. Yet, for many years there were no children. When Abraham became one hundred years of age, God made good on His promise to Abraham. Years later, God instructed him to offer his son, Isaac, as a sacrifice. You talk about trust! I am certain after much "soul-searching" he went to Mount Moriah where God had instructed him to go. You talk about trust! He laid his son, through whom the promise of the future rest, on the altar, prepared to offer him up as God instructed. Then God called him by name, "Abraham, Abraham" (Genesis 22:1-14). God saw Abraham's trust and faithfulness. God, Jehovah-jireh, provided a ram to be offered instead of Isaac. You talk about trust! We may conclude that if he had offered Isaac, God would have to raise Isaac back again from death because the covenant promise made to Abraham rested with Isaac. Abraham trusted God. It is a matter of absolute trust. Still I will trust You, Lord!

In the Apostle Paul's letter to the church at Rome, he gave this insight: "For whatsoever things were written aforetime were written for our learning; so that we through patience and comfort of the Scriptures might have hope" (Romans

15:4). Therefore, I have learned to turn to the Scriptures for direction, especially during times of trials, tests, and temptations.

This present day is no different. The past year has been one of many challenges. God has taught me to put my trust in Him. The past several years of being a caregiver to Vera also had its share of ups and downs. It was and still is a learning experience, but, still I will trust You, Lord! I understand what it means to be a true servant of Christ by serving my wife during this journey.

Even though some days are tougher than others, I would not give up this course of serving her. I have to trust God amidst my serving, in all that I do. I continue to sing to myself, "Still I will trust You Lord."

Chapter 8

KEEP PRESSING

"I press toward the mark for the prize of the high calling of God in Christ Jesus." (Philippians 3:14)

As I consider this last chapter in this book, it is not the final chapter of our lives. I am sure there are many who are walking in similar shoes of being a caregiver or dealing with chronic illnesses themselves. I am what they consider a "baby boomer." According to statistics, people are living longer, and there is a great company of my peers who are retiring, many having some sort of affliction that accompanies aging.

In spite of statistics, one does not have to succumb to the effects of getting older. When someone asks how Vera and I are doing, I say that we are growing older gracefully. It is to this chapter I entitled "Keep Pressing." Just like "Count it all joy" was my signature in years past, "Keep Pressing" is my signature today.

There are times we will be confronted with what seem like an impassible mountain, a devastating diagnosis, or some other crisis. However, one can still press forward while undergoing the trials of life. You need to make sure your "corner man" knows how to advise you when faced with the rounds of living. Each of us has so many rounds ordained of God to experience, and I am so glad Vera and I have an all-powerful God in our corner. He stated, "With men this is impossible; but with God all things are possible" (Matthew 19:26b). I can "keep pressing" with that assurance.

When Vera was diagnosed with dementia, our world began to change; we had to make modifications, but we kept moving forward. There is no shame having an affliction; yet, there is an attitude of defeat that can lead one to depression. God has enabled me to adjust to caring for my wife, and I love it. There were and will be trying days, but I hear God's still voice saying, "Fear not for I am with you; be not dismayed, for I am your God; I will strengthen you, I will help you, I will uphold you with my righteous right hand." (Isaiah 41:10) So with those words of assurance and encouragement I "keep pressing."

The apostle Paul said, "Brethren, I count not myself to have apprehended: but this one thing I do, forgetting those things which are behind, and reaching forth unto those things which are before, I press toward the mark for the prize of the high calling of God In Christ Jesus" (Philippians 3:13-14). I said earlier, "When Christ is center, crisis cease." Therefore, we can keep pressing forward amidst the ups and downs of life.

Even now, I am sitting in the waiting area with Vera as she will soon see the neurologist, Dr. Shashy for a semi-annual appointment. She is an excellent clinician and quite thorough when tending to Vera. This is a semi-annual appointment. Vera may not do much interacting with Dr. Shashy's questioning, so I will update Dr. Shashy on how things have been and are presently. Vera's sitting in a wheelchair with her head tuck to one side, just relaxing. The wheelchair enables me to move her around more speedily. This is a modification, but she does not complain about it. I just want to be there in the gap to serve her.

God has blessed us to experience three score and four. Our steps are getting slower, but we are not stopping. I am enjoying this season, amidst afflictions, and still pressing onward. We serve a God who is Lord over all afflictions. Should He desire, I know He can removed Vera's dementia. In that He has not and has given us His grace, we still press on to honor Him through a life of faithfulness and obedience.

We can "keep pressing" because we know who we have believed and are persuaded that He is able to keep all that we have committed to Him. The afflictions of this life cannot compare to what is yet to come. This blessed assurance is the center piece of our lives. Jesus said, "These things I have spoken unto you, that in me ye might have peace. In the world ye shall have tribulation: but be of good cheer; I have overcome the world" (John 16:33). James said, "My brethren, count it all joy when you fall into divers temptations" (James 1:2). John further stated, "Beloved, now are we the sons of God, and it doth not yet appear what we shall be: but we know that, when he shall appear, we shall be like him; for we shall see him as he is" (I John 3:2). My friends, the Scriptures are our comfort, and we rest our cause and hope in the promises and covenant of God. He has kept all of His promises.

Paul and Silas were jailed for their faith. Beloved it was not a Hilton or a Waldorf. It was a Philippian jail and later a Roman prison for Paul. There was no air-conditioning, no restroom as we know it, and no toiletries that were convenient. As he endured the experience of prison, he was still encouraging the saints through his letters to "Do all things without murmurings and disputings" (Philippians 2:14). In other words, stop complaining and start praising!

I will praise thee; for I am fearfully and wonderfully made: marvelous are thy works; and that my soul knoweth right well" (Psalms 139:14). Sin entered the world because of the first Adam's rebellion, and this awesome creation of God became subject to decay and dying. However, what the first Adam lost in the garden, the Second Adam, the Lord Jesus Christ, gained back! Hallelujah! Thus, he was raised on the third day according to the Scriptures with all authority and power, exiting the grave with a resurrected body. Therefore, these bodies of ours which have been subject to dementia, cancer, aging, death, and any other affliction, will be renewed! Jesus had a resurrected body and as believers in Jesus Christ, we will receive a body just like Him. So I can count it all joy and keep pressing because of this promise. This fact is the apex and zenith for the life of a child of God. So come what may, I say bring it on, for God has promised that He will make all things new!

Therefore, as Vera and I continue on this journey, we trust in the omniscient, omnipotent, omnipresent, unchangeable God to order and direct our steps. As she and I keep pressing to the high calling of God in Christ Jesus and walk together side by side, hand in hand, we thank and praise God. We do "count it all joy."

CPSIA information can be obtained at www.ICGtesting.com
Printed in the USA
LVOW07s0737261114

415616LV00004B/5/P